# LEARNING A LANGUAGE ALONE

# LEARNING A LANGUAGE ALONE

BY

D. S. PARLETT

LONDON
SIR ISAAC PITMAN & SONS LTD.

*First published* 1968

SIR ISAAC PITMAN & SONS Ltd.
PITMAN HOUSE, PARKER STREET, KINGSWAY, LONDON, W.C.2
PITMAN HOUSE, BOUVERIE STREET, CARLTON, VICTORIA 3053, AUSTRALIA
P.O. BOX 7721, JOHANNESBURG, TRANSVAAL, S. AFRICA
P.O. BOX 6038, PORTAL STREET, NAIROBI, KENYA
PITMAN PUBLISHING CORPORATION
20 EAST 46TH STREET, NEW YORK, N.Y. 10017
SIR ISAAC PITMAN & SONS (CANADA) Ltd.
PITMAN HOUSE, 381–383 CHURCH STREET, TORONTO

SBN:   273   42049   6

MADE IN GREAT BRITAIN AT THE PITMAN PRESS, BATH
F8—(F.148)

To my brother

GRAHAM

for learning Icelandic

# PREFACE

The purpose of *Learning a Language Alone* is to offer practical
assistance to those who wish to learn a foreign language in the
cheapest and simplest way—from a textbook.

A frequent and not unjustified complaint is that the cheapest
and simplest way is not necessarily the most efficient nor the most
effective. The present work is written from the viewpoint that
efficiency in the task of language-learning may be procured without
difficulty by the intelligent learner, regardless of the quality of the
materials to hand.

Few language textbooks are ideal. Some are written by linguists
with a fine grasp of the language but insufficient teaching experience to put it across; others are written by qualified teachers with
insufficient learning experience to put themselves in the place of
pupils they have never met, or to realize that the preparation of a
textbook requires a fundamentally different approach from the
preparation of a lesson. The first task of the learner is to understand
his problem; the second is to adopt a critical approach to textbooks
and to establish whether or not the writer has understood *his*; the
third is to make the best possible use of the material provided.

However far short of perfection textbooks may fall in their presentation of raw language material, the one valuable feature which
they are bound to have in common is that they present any material
at all. View your textbook, therefore, in its capacity as a servant: it
can provide you with much useful information. But don't let it become
a master by dictating the terms on which you should avail yourself of
its services: it does not know you as a person, and it cannot know
which particular problems of language-learning are likely to affect
you most.

The first part of this book introduces you to many of the problems
which are sure to confront you, and the second is intended to help
you solve them. It assumes that you have access to the raw material
of the language you want to learn, in the form either of a textbook
or of a grammar and dictionary, and also suggests the use of a record-
player and a tape recorder, although these are not regarded as
essential.

What *is* essential is that you should know what you are about,
and have the determination to pursue your objective wisely.

# CONTENTS

*Preface* . . . . . . . . . vii

## PART I: BACKGROUND AND APPROACH TO LANGUAGE LEARNING

CHAPTER        PAGE

1. Introductory—Plan of Work . . . . . 3

2. On Different Languages . . . . . . 7

3. On Language Differences . . . . . . 13

4. Learning—The Problems . . . . . . 27

5. Learning—The Methods . . . . . . 33

6. Learning—The Materials . . . . . . 40

## PART II: THE PRACTICE OF LANGUAGE LEARNING

7. Use of Textbook—Sentence Pattern Method . . . 53

8. Use of Textbook—Question and Answer Method . . 61

9. Use of Periodicals . . . . . . . 65

10. Use of Records and Tape . . . . . . 68

11. Use of Phonetics . . . . . . . 73

12. Use of Grammar and Dictionary . . . . . 79

13. A Hundred Grammatical Terms Explained . . . 86

*Index* . . . . . . . . . 101

# PART I

# BACKGROUND AND APPROACH TO
# LANGUAGE LEARNING

# CHAPTER I

# INTRODUCTORY—PLAN OF WORK

PEOPLE learn languages other than their own for various reasons relating to business, pleasure, or practical necessity. Some embark on another language at an early age because it happens to be on the school curriculum, and the lucky ones achieve creditable fluency by the age of sixteen. The less fortunate may not develop any interest along these lines until they have settled down, and, turning to a second language of their own free will, find the new work a pleasure and make speedy progress. Yet others discover in language learning an enjoyable and profitable activity for their days of retirement.

How do they do it? At the present time, when "mass-media" is almost a vogue word, when adult education is the latest craze, and when many Londoners visit the Louvre and the Sistine Chapel before setting foot in the National Gallery, the answer is not hard to find. Those who are gregarious and do not mind going out on cold nights have access to evening classes and language tuition centres, while those who are not, and do, can stay at home and follow language series on television when they are in season. Conscientious objectors to television—there are a few left—may like to buy a set of records from the Linguaphone, ASSiMiL, or similar series of language courses; and finally there are the book learners.

Now the book learners, on the whole, must have a comparatively hard time of it. They may have resorted to books out of choice, perhaps because they can concentrate better in the privacy of their own surroundings, but very probably out of necessity: there are no classes in the vicinity, they cannot afford television, record-players, or language records, or they are learning a language which is not sufficiently important or popular to have classes or records devoted to it. Armed with dictionary, grammar, and—if the language is not *too* obscure—a *Teach Yourself* or similar textbook for home tuition, their problems are just beginning. And it is to them this book is principally, though not solely, addressed.

## PROBLEM I: LACK OF BACKGROUND KNOWLEDGE

If you have had no experience of learning a foreign language before, you may be hindered from making elementary progress by the fundamental strangeness of it. This remark is less fatuous than it may appear. Learning another language does not consist simply of learning one foreign word for every word you know in English: the differences go deeper than that. There is no universally acknowledged logical *way* of expressing any idea in words. To take a simple example, where English says *I am thirty years old*, French says *I have thirty years;* and where we say *What's that?* the French say *What is it that it is that that?* Translation from one language to another involves the translation not just of words but of whole ideas as well, and where common ideas are regarded in a different light linguistic difficulties are bound to occur. In addition, you may find that the grammar or textbook from which you are working makes use of grammatical and technical linguistic terms with which you are unacquainted, or which, perhaps, you have not previously needed to remember: these are not always explained on the spot but are taken for granted, and you have to carry out some research to see what it is all about.

The first part of this book is designed to meet this problem by filling in the background—about language in general, about languages of the world, and about the workings of language. This has been done before, but here it has been written specifically with language learning in mind.

### PROBLEM 2: LACK OF GUIDANCE

In order to make thorough progress you will need more practice than textbooks are normally able to provide in the way of exercises, and you will require some satisfactory method of marking or checking. If you have only a grammar (no book with exercises) you need to be able to construct exercises for yourself. In Part II of this book a method is outlined which will enable you to solve this problem by carrying out for yourself a lot of the work normally done by a teacher.

### PROBLEM 3: LACK OF STIMULUS

You learn a language best primarily by speaking it, for which you require a stimulus to say something; this is normally provided by a teacher or a native. To lessen this disadvantage of learning alone another method is suggested in the second part which enables you to simulate the circumstances of conversation, and also encourages (*a*) thinking in the foreign language; (*b*) instant interpretation rather than studied translation; and (*c*) plenty of practice in questioning (which is often lost in classes).

## PROBLEM 4: LACK OF PROGRESS-CHECK AND ENCOURAGEMENT

The only substitute for outside encouragement is self-confidence: this grows from awareness of progress. The methods described in Part II enable you to concentrate as much on the spoken as the written language, and it is by noticing the ease and speed with which you can speak without making mental calculations that you will be constantly aware of the progress you are making.

## LAYOUT OF THIS BOOK

Any book of this nature would claim to be essentially practical in approach, and this one is no exception. I have attempted to introduce all the possible sources of useful information and speech practice that may be available to the home learner, including textbooks, newspapers, records and tape-recordings, as well as other possibilities (e.g. films) which are not necessarily restricted to "home."

Part I contains two chapters which might be headed "Background"; the first is about languages in general and their distribution throughout the world, the second about the actual structure of language. In both I have dealt with the subject from the point of view of the learner, and not simply as a matter of interest (although I hope you will find these subjects interesting): the first has bearing on what languages you might be choosing to learn, and the second on what sort of difficulties may be encountered as a result of the fact that no two languages say the same thing in quite the same way. Chapters 4, 5, and 6 deal with the approach to language learning: how language is acquired naturally, what lessons can be learnt from accepted teaching methods, and, in Chapter 6, what material is available to the learner and which items are really essential.

Part II examines in detail how the material may be put to use. I have, in particular, gone into some detail in respect of textbooks for self-tuition, for these vary widely in presentation and effectiveness. Often the authors have forgotten that they are writing for beginners, and simply produce a complicated grammar; some give no hints about making the maximum use of the material they present, and provide few practical exercises. Finally, there is a glossary of grammatical terms which are often used but not always explained.

## METHOD OF WORK

How you arrange your learning sessions and how much you attempt to do is to some extent a matter of personal temperament.

Learning a language takes time, patience and mental discipline. The following notes, however, are offered as a general guide—

1. Learning sessions should be spread out as much as possible, so that some contact with the language is made every day. It is better to spend half an hour per night on the work than three and a half hours on one evening. A language needs to be absorbed gradually and not taken in indigestible doses.

2. Keep to a routine. Following the methods suggested in Part II, each lesson should consist of (a) revision of previous work; (b) introduction of new material; (c) practice of new material and integration of new with old.

3. Work methodically. Keep all notes and written exercises in a file. Vary the types of exercise followed in each session.

4. Do not attempt too much at one sitting. Keep your sessions of the same length if possible, concentrate on one point at a time until you are sure you know it so thoroughly that you can write freely in the foreign language without reference to a textbook, and when you feel tired or stale, stop, and turn to something else.

# CHAPTER 2

# ON DIFFERENT LANGUAGES

WHICH language are you going to learn? Presumably you have already made your choice, and probably it will be based on one (perhaps both) of two interests: interest in a particular language for its own sake, or interest in a particular country which you would like to know better through an acquaintance with its language, whatever that may be. Are you satisfied that you have chosen the right one? In the first case, it is possible that you are interested in learning a particular language out of sheer enthusiasm for the people who speak it and the culture it contains—Arabic, for example, or Japanese, or the language of a minority group, such as Kurdish or Basque. But you must remember that it is not always easy to keep up contact with a language once you have learnt it, apart from travelling in the country concerned; that a knowledge of Japanese is, quite frankly, of little practical use in everyday life unless you happen to be particularly concerned with scientific literature. No; if you are learning a language for the sake of the experience, or for broadening your general experience by getting to know people who follow a different way of life, better choose one that is of widespread practical value such as French or Spanish, or, if you are unlikely to be enjoying periodic world tours, the language of a near-by country or people whom you are more likely to be able to visit—Danish, Catalan, Portuguese, Irish. If you are concerned with a particular country which you are likely to be visiting regularly or for a long time, and are approaching a language because you want to be able to get around without an interpreter, consider again whether you have had still a choice of languages, and if so whether you have chosen aright. It may be that several languages are spoken in that country—one may be a major and important language which would be of use to you in other places and other circumstances, but again, the local language might prove to be considerably easier and quicker to learn.

## A LANGUAGE SURVEY

A consideration of the number and distribution of languages through the world provides some fascinating food for thought. The first point is that there are many of them—3,000 is a good round number which gives some idea of the range in which we might be thinking, although this is nothing like an exact enumeration and is made without reference to the exact definition of language and its distinction from "dialect." As it conveniently happens, the present world population is near enough to 3,000 million for the purpose of this survey. Statistically, therefore, there is one language for every million people—the population of Gloucestershire, or the actual number of speakers of a minor language such as Estonian. But the distribution of these 3,000 languages is far from regular. For a start, probably 750 million people speak some variety of Chinese, accounting between them for over one-fifth of the world population. It seems likely that a further 300 million speak English, so that these two languages reach at least one third of the world's inhabitants. A further eleven languages may each boast over 60 million speakers: Hindi, Russian, Spanish, Japanese, German, French, Arabic, Italian, Malay, Bengali and Portuguese. A speaker of all thirteen major languages would be able to converse with nearly two-thirds of the inhabitants of the globe, yet this barely scratches the surface of the total number of languages. At the opposite extreme, it is of interest to note that, according to a census of 1961, the total number of mother tongues spoken in India was 1,549, only 30 per cent of the Indian population (then 439 million) speaking the national language, Hindi.

This state of affairs renders the statistical average given above very misleading, for it is doubtful if as many as one hundred languages have as many as one million speakers each.

It is obvious that some languages are going to prove to be more "important" than others, and it will probably be thought that the more the people who speak a particular language, the more useful that language will be. The correlation, however, is not so straightforward. Different languages are important or useful for different reasons as suggested in the following paragraphs.

NUMBER. Chinese and Hindi are spoken by large numbers of people, because they are the languages of very highly populated areas, and because the linguistic tradition is strong in the same area—the history of Chinese goes back over 4,000 years—so that more people are likely to pick the language up at the expense of another, than to lose it in favour of something else: their borders continue to expand. Yet neither has much currency outside the home area apart from among its emigrants: Chinese is the language of China, Hindi the official language of India, and neither is really of great practical value other than in the home region.

EXTENT. Other languages may have fewer speakers, all told; yet these may be far more widespread. English is not confined to a particular area: it is the language of the United Kingdom, virtually the whole of the North American continent, the whole of the Australian continent and a large part of the Pacific territories, and of half a dozen sizeable portions of Africa. It has a foothold in the Asian continent particularly in India, where it is the second official language. Spanish is the official language of nine of the South American countries as well as of those of the central American "bridge," and is in fact widely spoken in the south-western United States, while Portuguese is the language of Brazil, the largest of the South American countries. Both are current in other parts of the world as languages of colonization. French is the major language of France and Belgium, and is of great practical importance in Switzerland and in the Canadian provinces of Quebec and Ontario. It is also widespread over much of Africa as a major and official medium of communication. In addition it maintains a position as a major cultural language in the western world, being taught as a first foreign language and available as a culturally international language over the South American continent and the whole of southern Europe, penetrating into Turkey, and being in any case a language of colonization in Syria.

LINGUAE FRANCAE. A "lingua franca" is a language which serves as a medium of communication over a large area in which a multiplicity and confusion of many minor languages are to be found. Three interesting examples are Russian, Swahili and Malay. The Soviet States cover a vast territory and include many cultural and ethnic groups, ranging in type from Slavs to Mongoloids, in size from millions to a few hundreds, in ways of life from industrial to nomad food-gatherers. Although the groups are contiguous and could be enclosed on the map by a single line, their unity is essentially political rather than geographical. The indigenous languages spoken over the region include Lappish (related to Hungarian), dialects similar to Turkish, and archaic speeches possibly connected with those of the North American Indians. All of these are actively encouraged and propagated by the Soviet government—some, indeed, have been saved from extinction, and at least one has become a living and literary medium as the result of post-revolutionary efforts in education and the preservation of minority cultures. Yet Russian is everywhere the official language of administration, it is taught in all Soviet schools, and has speakers throughout the length and breadth of the Union. It is the lingua franca, the linguistic aspect of unity.

Swahili is widely spoken and used as a medium of communication particularly in commercial life over the larger part of central and southern Africa. Here too is a multiplicity of peoples and speeches,

but—by contrast with the Soviet example—the unity is primarily
geographic, and to a large extent ethno-cultural. Swahili is one

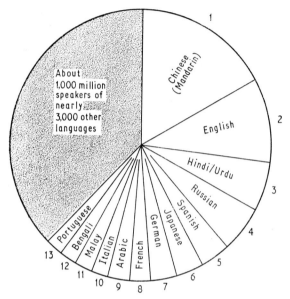

FIG. I. RELATIVE EXTENT OF MAJOR LANGUAGES

Fifty per cent of world population (over 3,000 million) account
for only eight out of about three thousand languages

of thousands of Bantu tongues, which together cover the whole of
the southern African subcontinent. Originating in Zanzibar and
the associated coastal region, Swahili has spread largely through the
business of trading as a lingua franca by which speakers of different
languages and dialects may communicate. It boasts 8 million
speakers, a poetic tradition of at least 200 years, and a growing
number of important newspapers and periodicals.

Malay occupies a similar position to that of Swahili. Its home
territory is the north coast of Sumatra, but it has gradually become
the most widely used medium of commercial and general communi-
cations in a region which includes the whole of the Malay peninsula,
southern China, Thailand, Indo-China, Java, Borneo, etc., and
in which some such lingua franca is also necessary as a large number
of languages and dialects have proliferated as a result of the physical
disunity of the area. It is the unifying language of an area which
is both geographically and to a large extent politically one; indeed it

has even been modified in some respects and re-termed "Indonesian" (Bahasa Indonesia).

It will be seen from these notes that some languages are of great practical value for large areas of the world where the language situation is basically complex and confused, and their value lies less in their numbers of actual speakers than in the number of languages they can replace.

What of the languages which are spoken by smaller groups, in more limited areas? Three groups might be distinguished here. At the bottom of the scale come those which, despite their interest to linguists and significance to ethnographers, are of no import to the world at large—the native languages of the Australian aborigines, for example, the near extinct language of the Andaman isles, or Ainu in the southern Sakhalin. Next to these we might distinguish a group of languages spoken by minorities within larger political states—Welsh, Basque, Provençal, Kurdish, for example—most of whose speakers, if not all, are bilingual in their native language and the major language of the state. These have their own particular interest, and some may bear the dignity of former greatness: both Provençal and Catalan, the former still spoken in southern France and the latter in Spain, and hence minor to French and Spanish, were major languages of civilization in the middle Ages—Provençal primarily as the medium of a fine and widely emulated literature, Catalan, with no mean literary tradition of its own, widely understood throughout the Mediterranean area as a language of maritime trade and commerce. Finally there are the modern languages which are confined to fairly distinct regions, the major languages of homogeneous states: Greek, Hebrew, Persian, Japanese—these are undeniably "great" languages, and worthy of study for their own sake, but only a practical proposition to the learner who is assured of spending time in their countries of origin.

## A QUESTION OF EASE

As we have mentioned, it may be that if you are interested in a particular country you will find that at least two and possibly more languages might be current, and you then have a choice. A good example is Switzerland, where French, German and Italian are widely spoken and understood, as well as the minor language Rumansch in the Engadine. You may then be guided in making your choice by the question which of the languages is likely to be of greatest use for other circumstances—solely from this point of view, Rumansch, for example, has nothing to commend it.

It may reasonably be asked, since we have agreed broadly that some languages are more "important" than others, whether some are also easier to learn than others. Again, the answer is, broadly speaking, yes. But we must be careful to ensure that we know what we mean by "easier." It would be true to say that a language is easier to learn the more similar it is to the one you habitually speak, so that the question of ease is relative, for us, to English (which is certainly not an inherently easy language for foreigners to learn). Thus Dutch, German and the Scandinavian languages would prove easier for an English speaker to learn than Slavonic (Polish, Russian, etc.), since the former are closely related to English (i.e. are descendents of the same parent language) and share a large amount of common vocabulary. The Romance languages (French, Spanish, Italian, etc.) also share a good deal of common vocabulary, and are in addition more similar to English than is German in respect of word order and sentence construction.

Some languages might be described as inherently difficult—by which we mean not only that they are objectively more complex and richer in grammatical distinctions, but also that they show features not found in any other language or language group, so that the speaker of any other foreign language would be bound to experience some difficulty in adjusting to the peculiar material. Caucasian languages possess an unparalleled profusion of distinct sounds and awkward consonant groups which must certainly prove a stumbling block to speakers of any other languages; Basque is notorious for its verbal inflexions; Semitic languages (e.g. Arabic) have a unique method of construction whereby most basic meanings are expressed by a set of three consonants, and grammatical distinctions made by varying the intervening vowels. On the other hand, Malay is by any account a "simple" language in that it lacks inflexions, and any word may be used virtually as any part of speech.

Finally we should mention the perhaps obvious fact that minor languages (Basque, Catalan, Rumansch) are not likely to be well represented, if at all, in the way of textbooks and dictionaries, and native speakers are difficult to come by away from their home territory. The difficulty is in finding the material from which to work.

The question of linguistic difficulties, however, is the subject of the next chapter.

# CHAPTER 3

# ON LANGUAGE DIFFERENCES

DIFFICULTIES are overcome by being prepared for them. Learning a language is not an easy task, if by "easy" we mean that it can be approached in a leisurely fashion, that things which are difficult can be muddled through, and those that are seemingly impossible ignored completely. However, to be forewarned is to be forearmed, and this chapter is intended to be a forearming as well as a forewarning.

The difficulties that necessarily attend the acquisition of a foreign language are of two sorts. First, those of the work itself: selecting material, adapting it into workable form, working and checking; learning, practising, revising; finding the time and maintaining the effort. A good textbook solves many of these problems, and it is hoped that this book may provide guidance through those sections in which a not so good textbook falls short of the mark. Neither, however, can be a substitute for mental discipline. Second, the purely linguistic difficulties of the material itself: both absolute, in that no language is free from irregularities and inconsistencies (none is "logical," few even apparently rational), and relative, in that every language has peculiarities of grammatical construction and style, even in respect of such lexical material (vocabulary) as may be of international currency or at least similar to that of English; so that learning a new language must demand to some extent the "unlearning" of your own. Learning new vocabulary is little more than a test of memory; acquiring a new process of thought and expression is a test of adaptability.

The greater part of this book is concerned with the former, since the problem of finding a practical method of work depends for its solution on experience which the learner simply may not have. In this chapter, however, it would be useful to consider the second problem by examining those aspects of the structure of a language in which purely linguistic difficulties may be encountered. In effect—how different can languages be from one another?

## SOUNDS

The medium of speech is sound, which is formed by the expulsion of air from the lungs, through the mouth and/or nose, and via the vocal chords. If the latter are allowed to vibrate the sounds are voiced; otherwise they are unvoiced. In either case movement (articulation) of the organs of speech (*see* Fig. 2, page 77) constantly interrupts the flow of sound, and different means of articulation analyse the flow into separate elements, or distinct sounds. Distinctive sounds are produced by different combinations of factors such as the shape of the mouth (position of lips and tongue), the type of movement of the speech organs, opening or closing of the nasal cavity, and so on. The possible combinations are virtually infinite, but of course the ear and associated part of the brain can distinguish a very limited number—even so this may amount to a few hundred in the case of a trained linguist. A language, fundamentally, is a code, and the elements of this code are these distinct sounds. For this purpose the range is far more restricted: most western European languages have between 30 and 40, though exact figures cannot be given without agreeing on the definition of a single distinct sound (the number given for English may thus range between 38 and 44). Extremes may be represented by the 75 of Abkaz (a Caucasian language), and the 18 of South Greenlandic Eskimo.

These facts have, of course, considerable bearing on language learning, since the degree of correspondence between the sound systems of different languages may vary to a large extent. It is not reasonable to expect that many, *if any*, of the sounds of the language you are learning will be identical with the sounds of English. Some will be completely new, others similar at first sight (or rather at first hearing) but in fact slightly different. Paradoxically, those which are new may prove easier to learn than those which have close parallels in English. Let us take some simple examples. In French, the nasal vowel sound usually written **un** can be produced by pronouncing the **u** sound of English **un** (in *undo*) through the nose, and without articulating the consonant **n**. After a little practice and guidance an English speaker can easily master the sound, although it does not exist as one of the distinct sounds of the English language. On the other hand, the French consonant **p** (in *pas*) differs very slightly from the equivalent English **p** (in *pa*), but the actual difference is difficult to make clear to many English speakers. The English **p** sound is followed, at the beginning of a word or between vowels, by a slight aspiration (the voiceless sound **h**); this aspiration is absent in the French **p**, so that it sounds much lighter to English ears—almost like a **b**. The reason why it is difficult both to distinguish and to produce is that it is so close to the English **p** that, when an attempt is made at it, force of habit automatically asserts the aspiration customarily found in English. In this case the English **p** is sufficiently close to the French to prove a distraction, a disadvantage which does not apply to the nasal sound **un** which has no such close equivalent. The difficulty is increased in some cases where a language possesses two distinct sounds both of which are similar to a single sound in English. Arabic, for example, has two consonants roughly equivalent to the English **k** (or hard **c** as in *car*). The two are distinguished when Arabic is written in Roman script by the use of **k** for one of these and **q** for the other. The **q** sound is produced further back in the throat than **k**, and great concentration is required when learning first to distinguish the two sounds, and then to pronounce them; for one cannot replace the other without possibly totally altering the meaning of the word. This situation may be better understood if you consider the case of a Japanese speaker learning English. English distinguishes two fairly similar sounds **r** and **l**; Japanese has neither, but does possess a sound which is rather closer to **r** than to **l**. Hence, when Japanese incorporates English words containing either of these sounds, they alike become **r**—thus *coal-tar* is *koru-taru*. In learning English, then, the Japanese must pay particular attention to the distinction between these two sounds, for his ability to make himself understood will be more than a little impaired by their confusion—he might, for example, *lead a wrong card* when he really intends to *read a long card*.

Differences and difficulties occur not only in the individual sounds of a language, but also in the total flow of sound—the rise and fall in pitch of the voice when speaking. When reading aloud from a passage of English we tend to lower the voice when a comma or a full stop is reached; in French the tendency is to lower the voice at a full stop but to raise it before a comma. More important, some languages distinguish between apparently indentical words by the tone of voice in which they are pronounced. Compare the two sentences: *Who did it? She?* and *Who did it?—She!* In both cases *she* has the same point of reference (feminine pronoun); in *she?* the voice rises, indicating that a question is being asked, while in *she!* it is lowered, indicating that the answer is being given. "Tone languages" actually distinguish different meanings by different tones. In Chinese, which is the prime example of a tone language, the word *she?* means *ten*, while *she!* means *city* (the phonetic correspondence is not exact, but is sufficiently close for this example). There are other examples closer to home, for even Swedish (which is fairly closely related to English) distinguishes some meanings by tone.

## WORDS

When you hear somebody speaking a foreign language you may recognize it partly from the peculiarities of some distinctive sound, but mainly from the accent and intonation—the total flow of speech, characteristic mannerisms in the rise and fall of the voice. The written language, however, reveals its character partly in individual letters (e.g. ø suggests Danish, ê French, etc.) but mainly in the form of its words. The word is the minimum practical unit of meaning, and words are the most obvious clues to the identity of a language.

"Word" is a conventional unit of division, and is difficult to define with any degree of precision. Few languages contain words which, like English *must*, are fixed and invariable in form—most have a grammatical system whereby words are modified in particular circumstances, for example by the addition of an ending or a change in one of the component sounds/letters. Such modifications are called flexions or inflexions. (Languages which make great use of them are referred to as *inflected* or *synthetic*, while those that use them to a less extent are, by comparison, *analytic*; we shall speak of these later.) They may be seen, for example, in the series *plays*, *played*, *playing*, all of which are words based on the stem *play*, which is in itself also a word. Another type of flexion is seen in *sing*, *sang*, *sung*, all of which are words based on the stem *s–ng*, although the latter cannot be classed as an independent word.

We are, however, digressing, in so far as we are discussing a definition of the word *word*: suffice it to say that, although it might be more precise to talk about roots and stems and flexions, *word* is readily understandable as a unit to speakers of most languages, certainly in Europe, and is therefore good enough for all practical purposes. What *is* both relevant and worth underlining is that words are rarely fixed and static elements with exact correspondences and counterparts between different languages. The most elementary howlers can be perpetrated through automatically looking in a dictionary for the first available equivalent of an English word in a foreign language. I have recollections of a schoolboy who, wishing to translate into French *I saw my brother*, looked up *saw* and found the verb *scier*. First he wrote down *Je scie mon frère*, which made him either a good magician or a homicidal maniac. Then he remembered that *saw* was the past tense of *see*. His realization did not go far enough, however, for, instead of looking up *see* to find the past tense, he assumed that *Je scie* meant *I see* (the verb being pronounced much the same in both cases). So he simply put *scier* into the perfect tense and produced *J'ai scié mon frère*. Having thus sawn his brother in half he felt linguistically fulfilled. No; learning a language consists only partly in learning a set of new words—much of the work involves learning their correct form and function in particular circumstances.

## FORM OF WORDS

Dealing with form first, what correspondences are likely to be found between foreign words and their English counterparts? The greatest similarities are to be expected in the realm of technical terms, in the broadest sense of the word "technical": thus, for example, the word *radio* is common in that form to most languages of Europe, and the word for *car* will generally be found in the same form as the abbreviated American *auto*. Amongst the languages of Europe a large degree of correspondence will be found in respect of concepts attributable to a common culture, for example, music, history, literature, biology, etc. The reasons for such similarities are not hard to find. In the first place, a large amount of vocabulary has been deliberately created during the last hundred years or so for concepts and phenomena introduced by the growth of science and technology. Since existing terms are generally insufficient, new words have been formed on the basis of material from the classical languages, Greek and Latin. Thus *television* is derived from Greek *tele* = *far* and *vision* from Gallicized Latin = *sight*; to this class belong also *telephone, telegraph, photograph, photogen,* and hundreds of others. Some languages, notably German, prefer to draw on native roots to produce the necessary vocabulary, for example, German *Fernsehen* (television) is a literal translation of *tele* and *vision*. In the main, however, such similarities may be expected. Another point which strengthens this is the fact that words of international currency denote equally international phenomena; for cars, television, music, literature, and the others, are not the personal property of any one nation or national culture. Indeed, as invention continues to grow, material civilization will become less local and more international, and will inevitably result in the great increase of this sort of vocabulary. It is, however, important to note that the actual forms of these words as they appear in different languages tend to vary in accordance with the structure and orthography of native material, hence we find for English *historical* the French *historique,* Spanish *histórico,* Swedish *historisk,* German and Dutch *historisch.* Once you are acquainted with the flexions and spelling habits of the language you are learning you will often be able to make quite accurate guesses for the equivalent forms of technical words.

Other close correspondences are due to borrowing, and many such loan-words date from the centuries of colonization by European nations. Amongst words which have been introduced into European languages together with the introduction of the item concerned into Europe we might mention *tomato,* the Spanish form of the native Mexican *tomatl,* whose name has tagged along with the fruit wherever it has wandered, and the same applies to *tobacco.* As well as borrowings from native languages in all parts of the world for whatever items are foreign to the speakers of the borrowing languages, there are those arising from the production of a useful word from the stock of one language which others then find indispensable to their own lists. An interesting example is the deliberate compound from "Anglo-Saxon" roots *folklore*, apparently first mentioned in about 1846, which has found its way into some strange situations and forms, such as the French adjective *folklorique* and the Spanish *folclórico*. English has also produced many sporting terms that have been widely adopted—*football*, for example, appears as far away as Japan in the form *futu baru* (note the conversion of **l** to **r**). But instances of borrowing are not predictable; the borrowed words in foreign languages may come as a pleasant surprise to the learner, but few helpful generalities can be made in this respect.

Similarities of vocabulary occur as the result of regular sound correspondences amongst languages which are closely related, i.e. which represent historical developments from the same "parent" language, such as French, Spanish and Italian from Latin, or English, Dutch, German and Scandinavian languages from Common Germanic. The vocabulary concerned relates to everyday objects and activities, e.g. pronouns, numerals, family relationships, feeding, moving, perceiving, etc.

By far the greatest number of similarities occur in languages which are thus closely related to one another. As far as we are concerned, this means that in practice many words in other Germanic languages may bear a resemblance to their equivalents in English, while many in other Latin-derived languages will be familiar if you know French (though English is also of use here because 50 per cent of English vocabulary is Latin in origin, mainly through the influence of French). Knowledge of Russian will make much of the vocabulary of other Slavonic languages recognizable, e.g. of Polish, Czech, Serbo-Croat, Bulgarian and others.

Such similarities may not be immediately apparent, for the regularities are as much those of differences as of similarities. Let us illustrate the point. German *Zeit* does not immediately suggest English *tide* (which basically means, like the German, *time*). But the following series of correspondences explains the connexion—

| English | German | English | German |
|---------|--------|---------|--------|
| tide | Zeit | God | Gott |
| to | zu | brood | Brut |
| ten | zehn | broad | breit |
| tongue | Zunge | hard | hart |

From these it will be seen that there is a regular correspondence between English initial **t** and German initial **z**, and between

English final **d** and German final **t**. Again, correspondences between **d/t, v/b, t/s** will be found in the sets *drink/trinken, dance/tanzen; live/leben, give/geben; foot/Fuss, water/Wasser*. The relationship between English and German words stands out quite clearly in many instances wherever there may be found a series of words revealing the fact of an historical sound-change. In the Latin languages we find more instances; first the correspondence of Spanish initial **h** with French **f**, second of Italian **consonant + i** with French **consonant + 1**—

| Spanish | French | Italian | French | (and English) |
|---|---|---|---|---|
| hierro | fer (iron, cf. ferrous) | fiore | fleur | (flower) |
| harina | farine (flour, cf. farinaceous) | biondo | blond | |
| hija | fille (daughter, cf. filial) | pianta | plante | (plant) |
| humo | fumée (smoke, cf. fume) | bianco | blanc | (blank = white) |

Regular sound correspondences are, of course, only of use in language learning if you are already acquainted with a related language. Where they do occur, it is usually in respect of simple, everyday words connected with the home, the family, food, basic activities, and most of all they may be looked for in the pronouns, numerals and simple verbs. A knowledge of such similarities increases as you learn more vocabulary, and once you have noticed sufficient examples to realize the underlying pattern they will help largely in the comprehension of new words in the language you are learning. In many cases they will enable you to make fairly accurate guesses as to the form of words which you do not know.

## MEANING OF WORDS

A pair of words which are similar in two languages, such as *Zeit* and *tide*, are described as **cognate**. Such cognates do not, however, necessarily share the same meaning: in this case, for example, *Zeit* is the dictionary equivalent of *time*, while *tide* is represented in German by *Ebbe und Flut* (and here it is interesting to note that these are cognates of *ebb* and *flood*, while the original meaning of the English is still found in the phrase *time and tide*: similarly, *Zeit* is occasionally found, in poetry, with the meaning *tide*). German *Wasser* is both a cognate and dictionary equivalent of English *water*. This brings us to the subject of the reliability of dictionary equivalents, and an examination of the meanings of words rather than of their forms.

Words of the same sound or spelling but with different meanings are called **homonyms,** and one of the commonest sources of confusion is to be found in words which are homonyms or cognates in two different languages, but which do not have the same meaning. Consider, for example, the English and the French words *place*, which are both cognates and homonyms—

> Eng. place (= spot, situation): Fr. endroit
> (= seat, e.g., in a train): Fr. place.
> Fr. place = 1. Eng. square (e.g. market-square)
> 2. Eng. place, seat.

Since the English word *place* is such a conveniently imprecise word, most often used in phrases equivalent to *anywhere, somewhere*, its use in translations will most often require the French *endroit*, although the natural tendency is for the English speaker incorrectly to select French *place* because it is a more familiar word than *endroit*. Similarly, care is needed in the translation of the French *place*, for this will often mean *square* (it is, incidentally, cognate with Italian *piazza*—note i for l—and Spanish *plaza*, which has also found its way into English). Such pairs of words are often called **faux amis**—false friends, for obvious reasons. Others include French *large = wide* (not *large*, which in French is *grand*, which can also mean English *grand!*), *monnaie = (loose) change, actuellement = at the moment.* The lesson to be learned is this: whenever you meet a foreign word which is identical or very similar to the English, be on your guard, and check in the dictionary. Beware of traps set by *faux amis*.

We need also to consider two other aspects of dictionary equivalents, occasioned by the fact that many words in any language may be used in different ways and with different shades of meaning. Some have connotations as well as denotations; some are used figuratively as well as literally. We shall deal first with the distinction between connotation and denotation.

The **denotation** of a word is its primary meaning. From this point of view the adjectives *eccentric, abnormal* and *perverted* have much the same denotation, descriptive of the state of deviation from a standard. The first is derived from Latin meaning *out of centre*, the second *away from the "norm"* (Latin *norma* = carpenter's square), the third, *turned through* or *away*. Nevertheless they all bear **connotations,** or secondary meanings, which reflect an emotional attitude on the part of the speaker. Thus, *eccentric* will be used as a sympathetic epithet in respect of a person whose quirks and oddities are the cause of a kindly amusement, while *perverted* is charged with a feeling of revulsion, and will be used in reference to behaviour which is unnatural or shocking. *Abnormal* stands somewhere between the two, and is almost objective, free from any associated value judgement. In such cases the choice of a word gives more information about the person using it than about the person described: the same character might be described by different onlookers using any of these three, according to their own feelings. Often a word may change its denotation as the result of its connotations or use in particular cases; thus *enormous* (which derives from roots meaning *out of the "norm"*) has come to have a more precise area of significance, in this case in respect of size, so that its primary meaning is quite distinct from those of the three adjectives discussed in the earlier part of this paragraph.

You may have noticed that the word *eccentric*, above, does have a meaning which is closer to the meaning of its roots, *out of centre*. An *eccentric wheel* is one whose axle is attached at some point other than its centre, and the path it traces in its movement is also eccentric. This, in fact, is its *literal* meaning, while its application to a person whose life revolves around some unusual centre of interest is entirely *figurative*. An unpleasant person might be described as a *swine*, a greedy one as a *pig*, and one who takes all the bed-clothes, or will not get out of your way on the fast lane, or will not let you have the middle section of somebody else's paper, as a *hog*. These, too, are figurative uses of words which, in their literal sense, refer to one type of animal.

It will now be apparent that word-for-word correspondences cannot always be exact, and the point is of importance in language learning. You will, for example, need a dictionary, and it is clear that a pocket dictionary will not be able to include many, if any, of the secondary and figurative meanings of words in either language. The connotations of particular foreign words will often be different from those of the nearest English equivalent given in the dictionary. This aspect of the use of vocabulary, the connotations of words in the language you are learning, can only be satisfactorily dealt with through constant reading when you have reached the more advanced stages: the comprehension of exact denotations and connotations depends on a sensitive comprehension of the whole context. The figurative use of words is easier to give if the dictionary is sufficiently comprehensive, but of course you have to take the initiative by being constantly on your guard against translating literally when the English is obviously figurative. If you tell a Frenchman "Vous parlez un tas de tripes" he will probably be at a loss to understand you, and if he concludes then that "Vous dites des bêtises," his will be an opinion rather than a translation.

## GRAMMATICAL STRUCTURE

While the sounds of a language are its most distinguishing mark at first hearing, and its word-forms the most distinctive feature at first sight, it is probably in grammatical structure that the personal genius of a language is most completely expressed. By grammatical structure is meant the systematic principles in accordance with which words are used in conjunction with one another to produce intelligible and unambiguous statements. The necessity for such a system is apparent as soon as we consider any set of words that might be formed into a sentence. For example, given the set *eat, fish, men*, in that order no coherent idea is conveyed: reference has merely been made to three ideas, two of which are of physical entities and the other of a general activity—i.e. two nouns and a verb. Rearranging them, we can produce either *men eat fish* or *fish eat men*. In both an intelligible statement is produced, but the two statements are different in meaning because it is clear that, in the first, *men* are doing this to *fish* (i.e. *men* is the subject, *fish* the object of the verb), and vice versa in the second. In order to produce either statement from the given words we follow two of the grammatical principles governing word-order in English—

1. The subject of a simple sentence precedes the verb.
2. The object of a simple sentence follows the verb.

It is clear that, without such principles, a combination of words would simply be a meaningless jumble.

In this example we see how grammatical relations (relation of subject to object in this case) are expressed by means of word order. But word order is only one possible method of achieving the desired effect; other methods are theoretically possible (not necessarily in English), and they include (1) use of flexions, (2) use of particles or "empty words." These three basic methods may be illustrated in the following examples—

English: Here is the woman's money.
French: Voici l'argent de la femme.
Welsh: Dyma arian y wraig.

The grammatical relation to be expressed in this sentence is that of possession: *the woman* is the possessor, *the money* the thing possessed. In Welsh (*arian* = money; *y wraig* = the woman) we see how this is done solely by means of word order. It is a grammatical principle of Welsh that possession is denoted by juxtaposition of the things concerned, and that possessed precedes the possessor. In English we follow the principle that possessor is indicated by the flexion **'s**: *woman's* is said to be the possessive case of *woman*, and must precede the thing possessed (so that, here too, word order plays some part). In French the nouns remain unchanged, but the grammatical relationship is expressed by means of a particle **de**—this is a marker, or functional word, denoting a relationship rather than bearing a meaning (hence the term *empty* word). The fact that **de** can be matched in English by **of** (*the money of the woman*) does not make it any more "meaningful," for **of** is also merely a marker word. That it cannot always be replaced by (and therefore be said to "mean") *belonging to* may be indicated by other examples of its use in English—

> the door of the house, a teacher of maths, a smell of onions, a matter of fact, born of the age we live in.

The extent to which these basic methods of establishing grammatical relationship are used in particular languages does, of course, vary considerably. In fact, it forms one basis of classification. All languages which distinguish separate words also distinguish rules of word order. In some, word order serves to clarify relations (e.g. in English to relate subject to object, in Welsh to denote possession); in others, it may do little more than to indicate shifts of emphasis (e.g. the house is here/here is the house); in some the order is strict and invariable, in others it is flexible. The actual order, of course, varies from language to language: in Welsh, the verb normally comes first, and the subject follows, for example—

> *Mae'r dyn hwn yn feddyg* (this man is a doctor, literally *is this man a doctor*—that is, Welsh statement order corresponds with English question order), but *Y dyn hwn sydd yn feddyg*: it is this man who is a doctor, that is if the noun comes first it is in order to emphasize the subject.

In German, the verb normally comes second in the sentence, preceded by the subject—

> *Jemand hält diese Karten*: somebody is holding these cards (word order as in English), but *Hält jemand diese Karten?* (verb denotes question) and *Hält jemand diese Karten, . . .* (followed by another phrase) denotes a supposition: If anyone is holding these cards. . . .

Most languages make use of some flexions, some to a great degree, a few not at all. English has few regular flexions—they amount to little more than **-s** to show plural number and possessive case of nouns, and singular verb in the present tense, **-(e)d** to denote past tense, and **-ing** to form continuous tenses (e.g. *doctor* gives *doctor**s***, *doctor**'s***, *doctor**s'***; *hope* gives *hope**s***, *hope**d***, *hop**ing***). French is also fairly free from flexions, at least in the spoken language (many are written but few pronounced). Finnish distinguishes fifteen noun cases, that is denotes by flexions whether noun is subject, object, possessor, etc.; Chinese has none at all.

Many languages also make use of particles, like English **of**, French **de**; sometimes these are used in conjunction with flexions, e.g. German *das Haus* (the house) but *zu Haus***e** (at home), in which *Haus* is attributed with the flexion **-e** denoting the dative case, required by the word **zu**. This may be compared with Finnish *talo* = house, *talossa* = in the house (flexion denotes "inessive" case).

We can broadly divide languages into two groups: those which tend to express grammatical relationships by means of flexions, and those which are comparatively free from flexions and therefore place more reliance on particles and significant word order. The former are described as *synthetic*, because the word and its grammatical function are synthesized into one form (cf. *talossa*, above); the latter are, by contrast, *analytic*, since the two are kept separate (cf. *in the house*). English and French are predominantly analytic; German and Russian mainly synthetic.* It is important to get an idea of the extent to which the language you are learning tends to either of these extremes, before you start work, by looking through the textbook or grammar—some idea can also be obtained by looking at a long passage of text: synthetic languages tend to have many long and few short words, analytic have many short (mainly particles). The more synthetic a language is, the more will it differ from English ways of construction, and the more care will therefore be needed. It must, however, be remembered that these two terms are extremes: very few languages are entirely synthetic or entirely analytic, most contain features of each type.

## Languages are not "Logical"

There is no inherently "logical" way of saying anything. All languages are the result of thousands of years of evolution and adaptation to the needs of expression, and it is not to be expected that any two will express the same idea in the same way. No grammatical relationship necessary for clear and unambiguous intelligibility exists in English that cannot be matched by Afrikaans, Afghan or Australian Aborigine, but the methods of each language are peculiar to itself. To conclude this already over-long chapter

* These terms are useful for descriptive purposes, but are here simplified. Finnish, for example, is properly described as **agglutinative,** which denotes a particular type of synthesis.

we shall take three areas of language construction in which items puzzling to the English way of thought may be found.

The first is in the realm of idioms or everyday expressions. In English, to express age, we say *I am a hundred years old*; the French equivalent is *I have a hundred years*. In English we say *I have a motorbike*, in Welsh *There is a motorbike with me*. *When in Rome, do as the Romans do* is matched by German *With wolves must one howl*. *If you please*, in Spanish is *as a favour*. Is it possible to say in any of these cases that one method of saying something is more logical than the other? Of course not—the purpose of language is to communicate, and if a given phrase regularly communicates a given idea in one language, then that phrase is effective. It is effectiveness of communication which should be taken as the criterion in the assessment of any language, and this has nothing to do with logic.

Secondly, there is the question of grammatical redundancy. We have in English *the white paper/the white cliffs* unevenly matched by French *le papier blanc/les falaises blanches*. The English definite article and adjective remain unaltered in any circumstance; in French, however, we see first that *les* (the) is in a distinct form indicating the plural, that *blanche* is also a change of form, and has a plural ending in addition. This is occasioned by the fact that words which describe or modify a noun must agree with that noun: *falaises* is plural in number. That *les* is also a distinct plural form may be justified by the fact that the **-s** marking plural in the noun is not pronounced—in speech, it is only from the article that plurality is understood. But what of *blanches*? It too bears an **-s**, but as this is not pronounced it serves no practical purpose. The fact that it is in the form *blanche* as opposed to *blanc*—and here the difference *is* discernible in pronunciation—informs us that *falaise* belongs to the set of words termed "feminine" as opposed to *papier*, which is "masculine." The concept of gender adds nothing to the meaning or function of the words (except in a few cases where two words with different meanings are distinguished by gender): it is a grammatical redundancy. English is not free from such peculiarities—in *the boy works/the boys work*, the idea of number is twice expressed: once in the noun, and again in the verb. This redundancy is made paradoxical by the fact that the same ending, **-s**, is used on different parts of speech with diametrically opposed meanings! Here, then, is a field in which the term "illogical," or better "inconsistent," is justified to some extent. Be warned that, no matter what language you are learning, such discrepancies are bound to occur, and will cause difficulty. Roughly speaking, it would be defensible to say that such grammatical superfluities abound more in synthetic than in analytic languages.

Finally, the question of politeness. This amounts to more than the perhaps obvious fact that all languages possess words and phrases which are taboo, and should not be used in certain circles, or the old chestnut to the effect that the French cannot bear to have the subject of feet discussed at the dinner table. Many languages, and certainly most European ones, have both "intimate" and "polite" forms of the second person pronoun, e.g. French *tu* and *vous*; some have as many as three. This causes difficulty to the English speaker, who sticks to the one form *you*—not because it is more awkward to remember several words and the appropriate verb forms that accompany them, but because the distinctions between the forms can only be fully appreciated, in the case of each language, by spending time in the country concerned and learning through social experience—the most dreadful *faux pas* can be committed through using the wrong form. Even native speakers are often in a quandary: currently the point is particularly tricky in Swedish, and Swedes often avoid it altogether by using a direct name, or a title (cf. English *my lord*, etc.). Wandering further afield, we may note that Japanese speakers make great use of honorific phrases, whereby even the subject spoken about may be referred to in different terms according to the relationship of the speaker to the listener.

Probably these variations of thought and attitude as expressed through the medium of language appear more difficult in the abstract than they eventually prove to be in practice. The important thing is to be mentally flexible: do not take English, or any idea of logicalness, as a yardstick by which to judge other languages. As we have said before, the most difficult part of learning a foreign language is the necessary process of unlearning your own.

# CHAPTER 4

# LEARNING—THE PROBLEMS

EVERYBODY speaks *something*. This is an observable fact, as is also the fact that nobody is naturally born speaking but that the practice is acquired in early childhood. Hence anybody who is not physically or mentally handicapped in that respect has gone through the process of language learning with success, and is therefore theoretically capable of learning another language. This may seem difficult to believe to a schoolboy fumbling with the intricacies of French verbs and unwittingly trying to learn a theory of grammar which does not apply to the language anyway, or to an English trader trying to pick up some Chinese in Hong Kong. Nevertheless, it is reasonably true to say that if the feat has been performed once, it can be repeated. Then why do not more people speak more languages? Isn't there a catch in it somewhere? Yes, of course there is, but let's approach it in an orderly fashion.

## OUT OF THE MOUTHS OF BABES, ETC.

Everybody speaks something because everyone is born into a language—into the language of his family circle, his *mother tongue.* His knowledge of the mother tongue grows with his knowledge of the world, and it is through the medium of that language that his knowledge of the world grows faster than direct experience would allow, since the collective experience of his family, his country and the world can be expressed in language and so transmitted to him. The growth of knowledge and his use of language go hand in hand, to the extent that the two tend to become confused: as a child he believes in the reality of fairy stories that are read to him because they are expressed in much the same words and phrases that express the reality of his surroundings. Gradually he begins to think in words, and language becomes part of his dreams. Albert Schweitzer, who was from early childhood bilingual in French and German, maintained that although he was fluent in both for everyday practical purposes nevertheless German was his true mother-tongue, since his dreams, both as a child and as an adult, were invariably in German rather than French.

The child's first contact with language arises with his first contact of memorable experience. From his earliest moments he will be subjected to the constant association of the *sounds* that we write as "mummy" and the *reality* of his mother, an association of the symbol (word) with the referend (thing) which is the fundamental of linguistic procedure. It will, of course, be some time before he has become sufficiently relaxed in his quest for food to be aware of this constant association, and has limbered up such speech organs as are necessary for successful mimicry of the sounds, but eventually the circumstances will be satisfactory and just conducive to the momentous discovery that calling out "mummy" is just as effective and a little less strenuous than screaming.

The process of "sound and thing" association continues to develop as long as the child is capable of distinguishing the sounds and the things to which they refer, and forms the concrete basis of his knowledge and use of language. In the early stages the vocabulary learnt refers to the most obvious and necessary aspects of reality, which are far from being necessarily restricted to concrete objects and their corresponding nouns—more important than, say, shovels and telephones are evident qualities such as *hot*, *nice*, *nasty*, and verbal constructions like *sssssh*, *drop it* and *go sleepies*. The combination of an intense curiosity about the world, a desire to understand what is being said around him, the association of sounds and things, the absolute necessity to make his desires known, the encouragement that greets his earliest verbal enterprises, produce in the first few years of his life an ability in language which, seen from the vantage point of maturity, seems little short of miraculous. Throughout this period the forms, the structure, and the inner workings of the language are acquired quite unconsciously. The child associates talking so closely with reality that there is no real distinction between the two: he has not found it necessary to inquire into the workings of the language, nor indeed to distinguish it simply as an individual but component part of the world in which he lives. At this stage it is possible to teach the young child a second language with little difficulty, for the new language becomes merely reality seen in a new light, and he is sufficiently curious, and eager to learn and to explore the apparently new paths of experience which the second language offers him. (Perhaps we should modify the words "teach" and "with little difficulty." Teaching should imply "introducing the child to the language," that is simply using the language in everyday situations and putting the child in those situations. Organized language teaching however usually adopts the reverse procedure and introduces the language to the child in such a dis-guised and formalized fashion that the child does not really know what to do with it. "With little difficulty" implies the addition "on the part of the child"; how much difficulty the teacher may have depends on his approach.)

## THE DECLINE OF NATURAL ABILITY

Thus we see that the *ability* to speak is inborn; language itself however is not "instinctive," nor is the predilection to any one language inherent. Language is part of a cultural tradition, and has taken millennia to develop. Cut a child off from the tradition, and it will not speak. If we could postulate two babies abandoned on an island before they had learned to speak, and imagine that they survive to maturity, we can be certain that any deliberately differentiated sound they may produce would do little more than attract attention, and certainly be incapable of detailed communication. Again, if we imagine a baby born to a Polynesian, adopted by Icelanders and brought up in the far north, we know that it will grow up to be a fluent speaker of Icelandic.

Put that Polynesian-born Icelander (or Icelandic-bred Polynesian) into school and try to teach him at the age of 12 the language of his natural parents, however, and a very different state of affairs results. It is at this age that the average English schoolchild gets his first taste of a foreign language, because 'it is on the curriculum of his secondary school. It is at this age too that the natural ease with which a language can be acquired begins to fade away. His language teachability is lessened by the conjunction of several factors. Imminent adolescence makes him self-conscious; he has lost the intense curiosity and most of the spontaneity of childhood and is less anxious to perform difficult feats in front of his fellows. He has begun to consolidate and classify his knowledge and become mentally analytic: the fusion or confusion of language with reality began to fade as soon as he became aware of purely verbal humour such as puns and *non sequiturs*. More often than not he lacks motivation—he learnt his mother tongue because it was essential to be able to express himself; this he can now do without the aid of another language, and its redeeming feature of novelty soon wears off if the teacher is not careful. He has developed "linguistic prejudices," that is, his mother tongue has become so deeply ingrained that he has developed the unconscious assumption that there is one, and only one, logical way of expressing any idea; this is an assumption which becomes quite conscious as soon as he begins to learn another language.

A "linguistic prejudice" is any habitual feature of the mother tongue which differs from the corresponding feature in the foreign language and asserts itself when the second language is being learnt.

For example, it is customary in English to place the adjective before the word it modifies (e.g. *a black jacket*). In French the procedure is usually the reverse (*une veste noire*). By the age of 12 the child has become so used to the English mode of expression that he will not only unconsciously tend to say, incorrectly, *une noire veste*, but also quite consciously argue that "French is stupid—it's much more logical to say *a black jacket* than *a jacket black.*" By this age, then, it is clear that his speech habits are so deeply rooted that he is prepared to rationalize them and defend them: they have become prejudices which hinder his acquisition of a foreign language. (The tendency also to translate French *veste* as English *vest* is of course a closely related problem.)

## LANGUAGE LEARNING FOR THE ADULT

This book is principally addressed to adults who wish to learn a second language, and it may well be asked, perhaps with apprehension, whether these difficulties increase with age. It is well known that with the passing of time the mind becomes less flexible for coping with new situations especially at the academic or theoretical level—in fact the rot sets in at adolescence. This means, in effect, that the linguistic prejudices which begin to develop at a comparatively early age will be more deeply ingrained, that they will be more difficult to eradicate, and that the new speech habits of the foreign language will be correspondingly more difficult to acquire. On the other hand, the prospective learner will be benefited by the motive of a conscious desire to learn, and by the realization (often hard to maintain in younger people) of the ultimate aim and value of the work involved. Motivation will be stronger because the decision to embark upon another language will be his own rather than that of the educational system that runs him.

If these pros and cons balance one another, the scales may be favourably tipped by the nature and extent of any previous experience of a second language. Any such experience, only if once half grasped and now half forgotten, will be of value in so far as many of the difficulties will not be entirely new. Such advantages operate on the mental level; it is possible that previous experience may prove to be of some emotional hindrance, especially if the previous knowledge was acquired under unfavourable conditions such as the exhortations of over-keen parents, the irascibility of under-keen teachers, or the dullness of archaic textbooks.

That the mind is less flexible with age is indicated in the case of a family that goes to live abroad and finds it convenient or essential to pick up the surrounding language. Up to about the age of eight an English child with no experience of the French language will acquire a basic fluency in the language in a matter of months from attendance at a French school. His parents, however, would not make such speedy progress. They may pick up enough phrases to get by, but are unlikely to become fluent without some conscious study and practice, and are never likely to achieve the perfection of pronunciation that the child will readily produce. For, while the parents' minds are less flexible and their English speech habits too deep, their child is still sufficiently flexible to be able to cope with all the new facets of experience opened up for him by the new language, he is young enough to be able to achieve communication through trial and error without self-consciousness, and, of course, his motivation is greater because it is almost a life-and-death essential to be able to join in the social activities of his age group. Picking up the language is little more than another game.

## Essential Features of Language Learning

The ideal of most language learners is to be able to speak a second language with the same fluency as the mother tongue, but, since this ideal is difficult to achieve, it may be subordinated to such lesser aims as may motivate the learner to approach such a task, such as picking up enough to get by for all practical touristic purposes, or knowing enough to be able to follow scientific literature in the original Russian, German and so on. For the latter, a dictionary and potted grammar as reference material should prove sufficient; for the former, there is no shortage of phrase books complete with "imitated pronunciation" of the *oo ay lar bureau der post sill voo play* variety.

For the broader aim, however, it should be remembered that learning a language is a different proposition from learning a particular subject the basis of which is factual information, such as physics or archaeology. The study of language may be an academic subject, but its *practice* is, strictly speaking, a habit, and the necessity is that of acquiring a skill rather than of learning facts. The speaking skill may be likened to that of typing, or of riding a bicycle. It involves the practice of certain physical activities—those of the speech organs—until their production becomes automatic, their performance an unconscious one. You do not learn to type by studying the mechanism of a typewriter, nor to cycle by considering the problems of weight, equilibrium and dynamics. Presented with a typewriter or a bicycle, you would learn to make use of it by setting to work on it, trying experiments, making and learning from mistakes. Paradoxical though it may seem, a language is learnt most effectively by speaking it, and one of the aims of this book is to show how this requirement can be met in the process of self-tuition.

# CHAPTER 5

# LEARNING—THE METHODS

ON the face of it there appear to be four ways of setting about the business of learning a foreign language—

1. Live in the country where it is spoken and pick it up.
2. Attend an evening class and learn it under direct supervision.
3. Buy a set of records published by a language record firm and learn it under your own supervision.
4. Buy a set of language textbooks and learn it under your own supervision.

Since the object of this book is to give assistance in the fourth of these possibilities, the others will only be summarily dealt with, during the course of this chapter. It will be instructive, however, to examine them in order to collect any information which might be of use in working from textbooks.

We may eliminate the possibility of living abroad as impractical, but not without noting some of the factors involved. From the previous chapter it should be apparent that the idea of "picking it up" is generally a rather forlorn hope, owing to the limitations of mental inflexibility—there are people who have a knack for acquiring a fundamental practical knowledge of a foreign language through being in constant contact with it, but even these would have more difficulty with certain languages which are particularly different in character and construction from English or other known foreign tongues. Here the question of similarity is important. An English-speaker who knows German well may pick up Dutch, which could be described as formally midway between the two, by a combination of listening and reading in the country concerned. Portuguese would be fairly easy to pick up for someone who knows Spanish well, since the two languages are very similar and to some extent their speakers are mutually intelligible. Knowledge of one Slavonic language would enable the foreigner to learn another with comparative ease, but, although related to English, German, Spanish, etc., the Slavonic languages as a whole are so different in character from these that even slight differences between the individual members would be more difficult to distinguish and relate. In short, "picking it up" is unreliable and if you have the opportunity to live abroad you will certainly find it necessary to reinforce the natural advantages of close contact with the language by some conscious study—which brings you back to the other methods.

Needless to say, travel or residence in the country whose language you know or are well on the road to learning is an essential to the improvement of fluency and comprehension. The more you already know, the more you will learn.

## Evening Classes

There are two drawbacks to learning in an evening class. The first is obvious: the more obscure the language you wish to learn, the less chance there is of finding a class devoted to it. Still, you will lose nothing by finding out. The second is that the teacher or the system used may prove to be ineffective, and this, unfortunately, you will not find out until you have paid the fee. I write from personal experience and the sum of thirty shillings out of pocket, having attended for four weeks (it was not worth continuing) a Swedish class where the teacher spent most of his time discussing Strindberg with a few literary fans. Out of a total period of eight hours I had the limited experience of producing fewer than ten spoken Swedish sentences. Should you find yourself in the same situation, it is advisable to drop the class and spend the time more profitably at home.

Though the material may differ, the methods of language teaching in such classes are of course the same as are available in secondary schools. The traditional basis of language teaching lies in a lack of system known generally as the Indirect Method, whose features are too insignificant and imprecise to be satisfactorily describable. (The term in fact is deduced from a system known as the Direct Method, which by contrast does have a specific aim and means of achieving it.) Most language learning performed in schools until the later part of the nineteenth century was of the classical languages, Greek and Latin. Both of these (bearing in mind that, for the foreign learner at any rate, Modern Greek is considerably different from Ancient Greek) are, to all intents and purposes, "dead" languages—nobody learns them as mother tongues, they are learnt and practised as only literary media. Consequently the object of teaching them lay not in encouraging everyday fluency but in producing an academic knowledge of the grammar and an ability to translate and to "compose" in either of the languages. Thus vocabulary and grammar could be taught, almost in watertight compartments, as sets of facts to be learnt by reference to original texts. When modern languages (principally French) were introduced into the curricula, the same approach was continued with the result that they were learnt as written rather than spoken languages.

The Indirect Method is still used to a great extent in present-day classes, despite many advances that have been made during the course of the century in the field of language teaching. Briefly it may be said to encourage the learning by rote of lists of vocabulary and rules (and exceptions) of grammar, and the formation of sentences by formulae derived from these rules. The production by the pupil of coherent statements is then hoped for more or less as a by-product of these mental contortions. Doubts about the efficacy of the method are aroused by the number of people who after six or seven years of French or German boast themselves unable actually to say anything in either. Fortunate pupils who have the type of mind that readily assimilates grammatical principles (often they prove to be strong also in mathematics or chess) come off best here because they can safely turn their attention to the spoken word while others are still grappling with the theory. It is interesting to note too that formalized French grammar as it appears in textbooks (especially in textbooks by French academics) represents in fact an attempt to push the French language into the framework of Latin and Greek grammar, which does not suit it at all. Most of the practical work involved consists of written translations, as for school and public examinations. This fact itself pushes the business of speaking a language into the background—oral work, often incorrectly treated as almost a totally different subject from the theoretical material, takes place on a few separate occasions—so that even those who achieve a high standard in written examinations find themselves like their fellows, as I forget who once admirably expressed it, "grammatically competent to say nothing."

Reaction against this method resulted in the early part of the century in the Direct Method. Ideally, in its pure form, exponents of the Direct Method plunge their pupils more or less *in medias res* by speaking the new language from the outset and guiding and encouraging responses from the class in the same medium. The learning of grammar and vocabulary is dispensed with as a conscious activity, and the language is taught as far as possible through the medium of itself—a feat which resembles an attempt to start a car in top gear. The teacher needs to be above the run of mortal beings— the purists, in fact, tend to be fanatical to the point of insanity—and progress at first is necessarily slow. In the long run it certainly does prove to be more effective in producing a state of bilingualism, but in this respect it suffers from a fault diametrically opposed to that of the Indirect Method, namely that, although the pupils may eventually speak the language fluently, they are less able to write it with sufficient accuracy to pass school and university examinations, which, as we have noted, are, at present, predominantly written.

Other methods have also been proposed and practised with varying degrees of success, but the most significant development in language learning in recent years has been the growth of language laboratories—not as a method, although, as we shall see, their use necessitates a new outlook on the presentation of material, but as a means to supplement and reinforce classwork. In the laboratory, each pupil occupies a soundproof booth equipped with an individual two-track tape-recorder. Guided by the pre-recorded master track (which he cannot erase in the booth) he practises what might be called "sentence drills" which are recorded as he does so on the student track: this can then be played back and compared with the correct versions given on the master track. Each pupil therefore works at his own speed, making and correcting his mistakes in comparative privacy. The teacher operates a master booth from which he can either communicate with the whole class or connect himself with each booth in turn to listen and to guide its occupant.

"Sentence drill" is rather a vague term, but it does suggest the main feature of many types of exercise that may be practised in the laboratory, to wit, insistence on the practice of complete sentences rather than on the swotting of individual items such as appear in vocabulary lists and grammar résumés. The laboratory method brings home the importance of the differences—and relative values —between oral and written work. For example, in the classroom it is possible to set an exercise whose instructions may be "Write in the plural: *der Mann, die Frau, das Haus*," or "Give the correct form of the verb: *Les garçons (être) stupides*," which may, for what they are worth, be quite happily written down, corrected, and soon forgotten; in the laboratory, on the other hand, the work is entirely oral, and speech does not actually consist of strings of separate words and parts of verbs. The object is to *use* the various parts of speech in the context of complete and sensible statements, and most language laboratory exercises are based on this principle rather than on the tradition of textbook problems.

A language laboratory exercise requires the production of complete spoken sentences by the pupil, and is based on the principle that by repeating a number of sentences which follow the same basic pattern (order of words, e.g. subject, verb, object, and rise and fall of voice) but which differ from sentence to sentence only in elements of particular vocabulary, the pupil will be both learning vocabulary effectively because it is being learnt in use and not in the abstract, and acquiring an awareness of the rhythm and flow of the language which is an essential prerequisite to thinking in the foreign language. To achieve this, the pupil requires some sort of guiding stimulus so that he will understand what sentences are required, and, of course, the provision of a correct version so that he may compare his attempts until they coincide satisfactorily. These stimuli appear on the master track, and the whole process of a particular drill may be described as one of "stimulus and response."

Several different types of exercise may be given according to the type of stimulus used. The following sequence gives some idea of the techniques available, and the fact that the same responses are used in each case is to draw attention to this point.

1. Interpretation (Instruction: say in French).

| | |
|---|---|
| We are working in the room. | Nous travaillons dans la salle. |
| We are working in the garden. | Nous travaillons dans le jardin. |
| We are playing in the garden. | Nous jouons dans le jardin. |
| We are playing in the street. | Nous jouons dans la rue. |

2. Substitution (Instruction: repeat the first sentence, then substitute the given words).

| *Stimulus* | *Response* |
|---|---|
| Nous travaillons dans la salle. | Nous travaillons dans la salle. |
| Le jardin . . . | Nous travaillons dans le jardin. |
| Jouer . . . | Nous jouons dans le jardin. |
| La rue . . . | Nous jouons dans la rue. |

3. Modification (Instruction: give these sentences in the negative).

| *Stimulus* | *Response* |
|---|---|
| Nous travaillons dans la salle. | Nous ne travaillons pas dans la salle. |
| Nous travaillons dans le jardin. | Nous ne travaillons pas dans le jardin. |
| Nous jouons dans le jardin. | Nous ne jouons pas dans le jardin. |
| Nous jouons dans la rue. | Nous ne jouons pas dans la rue. |

4. Question and Answer (Reply to the questions in the negative).

| *Stimulus* | *Response* |
|---|---|
| Travaillons-nous dans la salle? | Non, nous ne travaillons pas dans la salle. |
| Travaillons-nous dans le jardin? | Non, nous ne travaillons pas dans le jardin. |
| Jouons-nous dans le jardin? | Non, nous ne jouons pas dans le jardin. |
| Jouons-nous dans la rue? | Non, nous ne jouons pas dans la rue. |

Points to note are that in practice, of course, a sample stimulus-and-response is given in addition to the instruction, so that the pupil is quite clear about what is expected, and that after a suitable interval has elapsed for the pupil's response the correct version is given (on the master-track) which is then repeated by the pupil whether or not he produced it correctly the first time. It will also be noted that there is a large amount of repetition of the same elements of vocabulary both in the stimuli and in the responses, so that the pupil is constantly in active contact with the material and so has more opportunity thoroughly to assimilate it, but at the same time he is having to make conscious changes which prevent him from simply repeating material parrot-fashion. And, of course, if the voice on the stimulus- or master-track is that of a native the immediate advantages are obvious.*

As I made clear at the beginning of the chapter, this brief survey of language-teaching methods is given with the object of finding features that may be suitable for methods of self-tuition. It is clear that the Direct Method offers nothing to the home learner since it is entirely dependent on the guidance of a teacher. Obviously record courses cannot overcome this problem, since the contact between teacher and pupil needs to be live. Such principles as may be discernible in the Indirect Method generally form the basis of textbooks for self-tuition, and as such they have the same fault of complete concentration on the written language. Very few suggest means of turning written exercises into opportunities for oral practice, while very many spend too much time on an exposition of the grammar and too little on the provision of exercises and connected texts illustrating actual use of the material given. A great deal is to be learned however from the ideas underlying language laboratory principles and the methods associated with them.

In order to appreciate this we should examine more closely the practical aims of language learning. In respect of the spoken word the learner will want to express himself in the language and to follow it when spoken by natives. If these aims are satisfactorily achieved he may expect also to some extent to be able to interpret, that is to relate freely in his mother tongue information communicated in the second language, and vice versa. As for the written word, he will want to be able to write what he can speak and to read what others have written, and if these are satisfactorily achieved then he may be able to produce a fair written translation. In tabular form then the aims are—

| *Oral* | Speak | Comprehend | Interpret |
| *Written* | Write | Read | Translate |

* This treatment of linguistic material can be used very effectively in the classroom whether or not a laboratory is available, and in fact forms the basis of the Bilingual Method of language teaching developed by Mr. C. J. Dodson.

The Indirect Method concentrates largely on reading passages and written translations, the Direct on speaking and following, that is, participating in conversation. The relative merits of these methods depend on the importance attached respectively to the written and the spoken word. Now it will be appreciated that reading, writing and translating are private activities, in the course of which the learner is performing a calculating exercise at his own speed. Speech however is a much faster process, and concentration on the written word at the expense of the spoken is of little help in the give and take of conversation, in which there is not the time to calculate. On the other hand, if the learner is encouraged to practise speech from the outset he will become more used to putting words together and forming sentences almost as fast as he can think of the ideas he wishes to express. If he then turns to writing the language the words and sentences will spring to mind faster than he can write them. In other words, speech has practical priority over writing.

Our object, therefore, will be to concentrate on the provision of material which, like that of language laboratory drills, is particularly suited to oral practice. All work must involve the elements of the language *in use*, for the most part in complete sentences, so that the language will be introduced and discovered almost entirely in the form in which it will subsequently be used. There should be no need to learn lists of vocabulary, or paradigms like German **der, die, das** (*see* next chapter), or rules and exceptions in isolation.

CHAPTER 6

# LEARNING—THE MATERIALS

In subsequent chapters we shall be dealing mainly with printed matter relevant to language learning, though a section is included on record courses and the use of a tape-recorder should either be available. By way of introduction we might summarize and survey some of the various sources of instruction and guidance that may be drawn on during the process of learning another language.

1. Textbook
2. Dictionary
3. Grammar
4. Reader
5. Phrase-books
6. Periodicals (newspapers and magazines)
7. Record courses
8. Radio
9. Films
10. Native speakers

Of these it may be said that the primary essentials are *either* a specific language textbook *or* a dictionary and grammar and reader. To be precise, it is essential to have access to a stockpile of vocabulary (dictionary), an exposition of the grammar, samples of continuous text (reader), and, if possible, exercises. Ideally, a textbook should contain all this material, but if the vocabulary it gives is insufficient in quality and quantity, or if it fails to give passages of continuous text, then these deficiencies should be made up with a dictionary and reader.

Now let us examine these items in greater detail.

### TEXTBOOKS

If you are fortunate enough to have a choice of textbooks for the language you are studying, as you will with major languages especially of Europe, you would be well advised to look through those available and consider their usefulness to some extent by reference to the following hints before buying one.

General points: note the original date of publication and those of subsequent revised editions. It would take too much space to say to what extent certain languages have undergone reforms of spelling and even of grammar and style during the course of this century: Norwegian and several Slavonic languages, including Russian, spring immediately to mind. Older textbooks tend to be too academic and theoretical, a criticism which does not imply that newer textbooks are automatically superior in this respect. On the other hand, one which has undergone a large number of reprints will probably prove to have passed the test of practicability and popularity. Broadly speaking, it may be safe to recommend avoidance of anything earlier than 1920, and preference for the latest editions of well-tried works, but a final judgement can only be made after consideration of more specific pros and cons given below. Note the length of the chapters: bearing in mind that books vary in size and format, an average of three pages (six sides) should be ample for each lesson, with at least one-quarter of this space devoted to practical work (examples, text, exercises). If the chapters tend to be in excess of this amount there are at least two possible reasons: either the grammatical exposés give far too much detail and concentrate on irregularities and exceptions to the "rule," in which case the book should be avoided, or a large number of different grammatical points may be covered at one time, in which case it will be possible to perform your own selection of material for any one lesson to avoid biting off more than you can chew. Finally note how vocabulary is given. Twenty words and phrases are quite sufficient for any one chapter or section, and should be specifically listed rather than scattered about the chapter. At the back of the book there should be an English-Foreign and a Foreign-English key, or at least the former. In particular, words given in the "Foreign" list should include information as to gender, plural of nouns, principal parts of verbs, or reference notes relating the word to a chapter or grammatical key which illustrates its correct use. If such a vocabulary is missing, then a dictionary will be at first useful, and soon necessary.

Specific points: an introductory chapter is desirable, giving both background information about the language (geographical extent, dialectal divisions, standardization, political and cultural status) and a survey of its principal features, especially those which are strange to English and other well-known languages (e.g., mutation in Celtic languages, verbal aspects in Slavonic, consonantal basis of Semitic, tones of Chinese, honorifics of Japanese, etc.). Some reference should be made to the system of spelling or transliteration especially if a non-standard form is used. An introduction to the phonetics of the language is usually given and can be quite valuable if the International Phonetic Alphabet is used (I.P.A., *see* page 76), but tread cautiously here: any sort of "imitated pronunciation" of the type quoted on page 31, which merely shows how the correct sounds can be roughly approximated by using the nearest English equivalent, should be avoided; also, the phonetics should be studied not in the abstract before starting the work, but in conjunction with the chapters as they are followed. In any case it is impossible to acquire an exactly correct pronunciation from the printed word—but more of this later.

Ideally (or so it seems to me) each chapter should consist of (1) a reading passage of connected sentences, (2) a discussion and exposé of the grammatical points introduced in it, plus a list of the new vocabulary, and (3) exercises based on them. Most textbooks for self-tuition, however, dispense with the first item. Some introduce continuous passages at a later stage, and many leave them to what is virtually a supplement following the instructive chapters. This procedure suggests that the authors are incapable of writing a simple text using the fundamentals of the language and reflects poorly on their qualities as guides to language learners.

The grammatical explanations should refer to one or two major points and one or two minor points at most, but here of course it is difficult to make precise suggestions since so much depends on the strangeness of the language and the difficulty of the points concerned. In this connexion, look for clarity of expression and guidance (at some point in the book) to grammatical terms involved—obviously you must readily understand what the writer is talking about! Look also for plenty of clear examples and illustrations of the points concerned using vocabulary that has been introduced and learnt in earlier lessons, and be very wary of an author who simply gives large tables of paradigms with instructions to learn them by heart, and dwells to a morbid extent on irregularities and exceptions. (As an example of the former, we shall have occasion to see later that there is no need to learn this paradigm for the definite article in German—

|       | M   | F   | N   | P   |
|-------|-----|-----|-----|-----|
| Nom.  | der | die | das | die |
| Acc.  | den | die | das | die |
| Gen.  | des | der | des | der |
| Dat.  | dem | der | dem | den |

It may, of course, be handy for reference purposes, but, paradoxically, nothing will be learnt from learning it as it stands.)

The vocabulary should be brought together at some place in the chapter, and should include all new words introduced in the reading passage (if any), the grammatical examples and illustrations, and the exercises. A commendable point is the relevance of the vocabulary to some particular background theme to which the reading passage and exercises may be related, for example *at the office, at the station, in the shops* and so on. If each chapter deals with one such theme, the consistency and coherence this imparts will help the memory in respect of vocabulary. A similar good point is the provision of "opposites," for example, if you are given the words for *big, fat, short,* you might as well be given also those for *small, thin, tall* at the same time.

The exercises should consist of separate sentences and sometimes of connected sentences in a continuous passage, some for translation from and some into English. Two main points to look for: separate sentences should consist of complete sentences and not just individual phrases—that is for all practical purposes they should contain a verb\*, and there should be enough of them to cover all aspects of the grammar and vocabulary given in the chapter. Secondly, and this is most important, the sentences should make sense. This does not mean that they need be profound or formally complex—obviously, in the early stages you will need to be able to string together a lot of elementary vocabulary in order to get used to the basic patterns of the spoken word. But it always comes as a disappointment to the learner if after three or four chapters of what is bound to be initially hard work he finds himself still restricted to such awe-inspiring statements (here taken at random from a few textbooks) as—

> The boy is from the trawler,
> The rudder is in the water,
> Throw from you that knife,
> Our dolls are in their fields,
> They fetched the dog so badly that they died,

and, of course, the by now legendary "our postilion has been struck by lightning" (subject of a delightful ballade by M. H. Longson—see *More Comic and Curious Verse* published by Penguin Books).

One good point in the arrangement of exercises, particularly those that consist of separate sentences, is the provision of two exercises using the same sentences, one for translation out of and the other for translation into the foreign language, preferably separated by another section or exercise. Although it may seem that this allows "cheating," in fact the temptation is avoided simply because there is no point to it, while it has the great advantage of allowing

---

\* All languages distinguish some elements which have a verbal function, but some (e.g. Russian, Malay) do not express the copula (some part of "to be") in such a sentence as "the house is big."

immediate correction afterwards without reference to a key at the back of the book. Practical experience of Caradar's *Welsh Made Easy* convinces me that more is to be gained than lost from this system.

## DICTIONARIES

First, choosing a dictionary. Get one that gives equivalents both ways—Foreign-English and English-Foreign. Other elementary precautions include checking the date of publication (same reasons as those in respect of textbooks) and ensuring that the print is large enough to be legible and the arrangement on the pages quite clear, so that each entry is easy to find and clearly marked off from its neighbours. Don't be attracted by the provision of numerous supplements on such subjects as tables of equivalent weights, measures, money, etc., or potted grammatical points: the purpose of the dictionary is to provide vocabulary. The only really valuable addition is a geographical section, giving names of countries, capitals, etc., although some dictionaries incorporate these in the text. Such terms are important; if the dictionary does not give them, look for one that does.

Do not favour a dictionary which gives a high proportion of vocabulary that is technical, regional, highly literary or obsolete, for, unless the work is very large, it will suffer from the fault of giving too few alternatives for more common everyday words. For example, examine the following French equivalents for the apparently straightforward English verb go—

| | | | |
|---|---|---|---|
| go | *aller* | go into | *entrer* |
| go across | *traverser* | go off | *partir* |
| go away | *s'en aller* | go on | *continuer* |
| go back | *retourner* | go out | *sortir* |
| go by | *passer* | go under | *succomber* |
| go down | *descendre* | go up | *monter* |
| go forward | *avancer* | go without | *se passer de* |

Even this short list, consisting of a few phrases picked at random, and ignoring such compound and colloquial phrases as *to go one better, there you go again!* and *going, going, gone!*, do not represent one for one correspondences. A simple case is that of *go across: traverser* is the French equivalent in the phrase *to go across the road*, but there is also a verb *franchir* appropriate to going across a bridge or a frontier—and then what about the figurative *go across to the other side*, meaning "to change one's allegiance"? Again, *partir* would do for a woman who goes off without saying goodbye, but not for a bomb that goes off, no matter what it says first. In choosing a dictionary, then, look first at the number of variations given on such everyday words as *go, see, one* (numeral? personal pronoun? demonstrative pronoun?), *key* (of a lock? of a problem? of a piece of music?), and so on. The question is not "are many words given?" but "are there many alternatives, and are they clearly explained?" Finally, it is essential that the dictionary you choose should give sufficient information about each foreign word to enable you to place it in its appropriate grammatical category. If the language you are learning distinguishes grammatical gender, you will need to know whether the noun you are looking up is masculine, feminine, neuter, common, or whatever may be the case. In respect of verbs, it is important to know whether a given verb follows a regular pattern or whether it has irregular forms, and, if the latter, what they are.

In using the dictionary there are two points to watch. First make sure you are looking up the right alternative, even the right part of speech (do you want *lead* as a verb or a noun?). Second, always refer back to the other part of the dictionary so as to double check the word you have looked up. If for example you are looking up *cigarette lighter* under *lighter*, and find the unexplained alternatives *chaland* and *briquet*, reference to the former in the French section is likely to reveal the alternatives *lighter, barge*, to the latter, the alternatives *lighter, flint and steel*—from which you can make the correct deduction.

## GRAMMARS

A grammar is a guidebook to the structure of a language. In traditional form, it devotes one section to each part of speech, generally in the order nouns, pronouns, adjectives, prepositions, verbs, adverbs, conjunctions, interjections. Each section shows, usually in some sort of tabular form, the grammatical variations that may be undergone by the part of speech concerned (for nouns the distinction or formation of gender, case, number), and groups together elements that follow regular and predictable patterns (such a pattern is called a paradigm, as shown on page 93), followed by exceptions and irregularities. We need to consider the value of grammars from three points of view—

1. It is clear that a grammar is not suitable for the business of learning a foreign language as long as there is a textbook available. It would be impossible to learn all the elements and variations for one part of speech without putting them into practice in the

construction of sentences. Any language textbook which is of any use at all must from the outset give the elements of sentence construction using nouns and verbs. If there is such a textbook in existence, use it, and pass on to the next two points. If not, and if a grammar is the last resort, then turn to Chapter 12.

2. In the early stages of language learning, a separate grammar is not likely even to be useful if you are using a textbook, for the purpose of a textbook is to show you primarily how to use the language and so to encourage a practical acquaintance with the grammatical structure involved, whereas a grammar expounds the theory on a rationalized basis. It is easier to study theoretical grammatical principles against the background of practical knowledge, assuming there is any desire to do so, than to use theoretical knowledge as a stepping-stone to practical usage.

3. Since a grammar is a guidebook to a theoretical knowledge of the language structure, it is primarily a reference book. Hence, in more advanced stages, it may be useful as a means to consolidate and set in order the principles you have been following, particularly if the grammatical sections of the textbook are not clearly set out. The important point to remember in using a grammar as such is that it should be used as a guide only to forms and procedures that you already know, or to give a brief introductory survey of items which you are about to study. There is no value in learning sections off by heart.

## READERS

At some stage in the learning of a language from a language textbook the addition of a reader will become highly desirable, if not essential. It would however be difficult to state categorically at what stage it should be introduced, since this will depend on such factors as (a) the type of reader available, (b) the extent to which the textbook makes use of connected passages of text, (c) the difficulty of the language.

As far as the type of reader is concerned, we may consider two, according to whether the passages or sections are "graded." In a graded reader, specifically produced for foreigners learning the language, the early passages will be based on elementary vocabulary and constructions, which will be gradually augmented and expanded as the book progresses. It will be of particular value if each passage is followed by an exercise based on straightforward question and answer lines relevant to the text, to be completed, of course, in the foreign language. If it is designed for English learners, the provision of a vocabulary with each passage would be advantageous, but this need not be regarded as essential. The purpose of a reader is to provide examples of the language used as a medium of communication without explicit concentration on grammar and vocabulary—it shows a language in its proper surroundings, and not as an object on a dissecting table. Hence a graded reader could be used in conjunction with a textbook right from the start; a method for use will be found in Chapter 9. If a non-graded reader is used, try to select a book which gives many short passages rather than a few longish ones—one page each should be quite enough. Most readers of this nature are produced for use in schools in the country where the language is spoken, and naturally presuppose a practical knowledge of it. You should look for one whose material consists of diverse writings on everyday subjects and/or short stories (e.g. Aesop's Fables are ideal, since the subjects will probably be well remembered). You should at first work from the textbook and periodically turn to the reader, but not make use of it until you have reached the stage where some of the vocabulary is recognizable and the underlying structure of the sentences can be immediately discerned. At what stage this occurs depends on the general recognizability of the language. If, for example, you already know French or Spanish and are learning Catalan, much of the vocabulary will be obvious from the start, and since word order and sentence construction are not startlingly different in any of these languages from those of English you should be able to make use of the reader right from the beginning.

## PHRASE BOOKS

The market abounds in foreign language phrase books, which, in their simplest form, do no more than to give everyday word for word and phrase for phrase correspondences and may as such be found useful if you are travelling abroad before knowing enough of the language to get by. To the extent that they do provide some raw material they may also prove handy as reference books, but they are not designed for language learning and therefore have no real place in your scheme of work. In particular many of them resort to the dreaded "imitated pronunciation" attempt which we have already advised against.

More ambitious phrase books include a potted grammar, which is no substitute for either a textbook or a proper grammar. I include in the phrase book category those more involved publications which promise everything short of life everlasting in a few months, and repeat, there is no substitute for a proper textbook or a grammar.

## PERIODICALS (NEWSPAPERS AND MAGAZINES)

Like readers, periodicals present the language you are learning in its proper surroundings and fulfilling its primary function. Unlike readers, some periodicals cater principally for the less articulate sections of the home market and may be written in a style broadly describable as "non-standard." These should be avoided. Choose in preference illustrated magazines produced with a view to sales abroad (the *Life* and *Paris Match* category), and *see* Chapter 9.

## RECORD COURSES

The obvious advantage of a record course, such as *Assimil* or *Linguaphone*, is that you become acquainted from the outset with the language as spoken by natives, and are so enabled to learn to speak with a satisfactory accent, provided you are capable of imitating it and spotting your mistakes. Nevertheless you cannot learn a language simply by listening to it, and all record courses are equipped with a guide or textbook to be used in conjunction with the records, which brings us again within the scope of this book. Chapter 10 is concerned with use of records and tape.

## RADIO

Assuming for the moment that there is an obtainable radio service in the language you are learning, and ignoring any radio lessons that may be available in it, we must admit that the wireless is not an ideal medium for any aspect of language learning other perhaps than for studying the flow and rhythm of fluent speech. If you are a good mimic, you may be able to improve your accent and intonation by bearing radio speech in mind when you are practising the spoken language. Otherwise there are two major difficulties to be encountered. One is that the speech, being produced for native audiences, will be too fast to follow unless you are already very well acquainted with the language. The other is that some sounds cannot be clearly reproduced by the loudspeaker—this applies particularly to sibilants (**s, z, sh,** etc.) and fricatives (**f, v, th,** etc.). When you listen to English over the radio these sounds are distinguished mentally because you know the language thoroughly, and the few sounds which are not in fact physically different as they emanate from the speaker do not prevent you from recognizing the sound patterns of complete words, phrases and sentences, and thereby automatically filling in the missing sounds. Unless you already know the foreign language thoroughly, then, you will not be able to distinguish clearly the words that are being produced.

## Films

Watching and listening to a foreign film can be an exciting experience linguistically as well as dramatically, for you feel yourself mentally transported to the country you are concerned with and find yourself set down in the middle of real speech situations. Unfortunately, this is only a feeling, and it is not likely to be of any practical value in learning. If there are English sub-titles you will probably find it impossible to ignore them. If not, and you know the language to some extent already, you will probably find yourself in a peculiar situation: the speech is too fast and too colloquial to enable you to follow it in any detail, and yet you are left with the conviction that you have broadly understood most of the dialogue. This is likely to be *not* because you have understood enough dialogue to follow the plot, but because the actions, gestures, tones of voice and background music have enabled you to understand the story and so misled you into believing you have followed the speech. When you have learnt the language, then following a film may help improve your feeling for the sounds and flow of the spoken language and perhaps increase your knowledge of colloquial forms. Until then their main value is in renewing or providing further incentives to keep at the job of learning.

## Native Speakers

These are handy commodities, if available. Use them for conversation practice, but find out—discreetly, of course, and preferably from suitably qualified third persons—whether they speak a fair approximation of the "standard," or whether their natural speech is a regional dialect. No advice can be given here if the latter is the case: it depends on how non-standard the regionalisms are, and to what extent regional dialects are socially acceptable in the country concerned. And unless they have had experience of teaching, it is not advisable to beg, bribe or bully them into giving you lessons.

# PART II

# THE PRACTICE OF LANGUAGE

# LEARNING

# CHAPTER 7

# USE OF TEXTBOOK—SENTENCE
# PATTERN METHOD

HAVING in Part I considered the reasons for learning a language and the materials we have available for doing this we shall in Part II consider how the best use may be made of our time and our opportunities.

## THE SENTENCE PATTERN

The quickest way of learning a language is to speak it, so the first requirement is to find as much material as possible for speech practice. In so doing, however, two extreme dangers must be avoided. On the one hand, you must not restrict yourself to too few actual sentences and learn these off by heart, otherwise you will only be able to produce them parrot-fashion and will have difficulty in applying this ability to new material; on the other, you must not attempt to practise too many different types of sentence bearing little relation to one another, otherwise your memory will be strained and your progress retarded. These dangers are avoided by producing sentences that have in common an underlying grammatical structure or pattern, but whose actual meanings can be considerably varied by changing the individual words of which they consist.

In the textbook for self-tuition in French which I now have beside me the first exercise consisting of complete sentences begins: *Les rues sont larges*, which you are required to translate into English as *The roads are wide*. Having done so, stop and consider what other sentences of this type you could produce using other vocabulary given in this chapter. Instead of *les rues* you could substitute *les maisons* (houses), *les villes* (towns) or *les voitures* (cars): thus there are four possibilities for the first element of that sentence. Again, as well as being *larges* these items could be *grandes* (big), *petites* (small) or *étroites* (narrow: this adjective is not given in the first chapter but appears in the vocabulary at the back of the book. It is of course a logical and useful procedure to learn adjectives in pairs of opposites, e.g. big/small, wide/narrow, long/short). Can the verb element (*sont*) also be changed? You will naturally expect to be able to say *the roads are not wide*, making the verb negative. This feature does not appear in the first chapter, which invites the suspicion that there may be something peculiar about it. A brief glance through the next couple of chapters shows that this is so: there are two words necessary to express *not*, and these go one on each side of the verb. Since, however, this is not a drastic alteration affecting the rest of the sentence as well there is no reason why it should be omitted from this type of sentence.

From this material the following sentence pattern can be constructed—

| les rues<br>les maisons<br>les villes<br>les voitures | sont<br>ne sont pas | larges<br>étroites<br>grandes<br>petites |
|---|---|---|

By writing the words out in that form you acquaint yourself with their meanings and spellings, but in addition you are seeing them not in isolation but as components of a whole sentence, which, after all, is what words are intended to be. It will be seen that this pattern consists of only ten different elements, i.e. four subjects, two verb forms, and four adjectives, yet from it can be produced $4 \times 2 \times 4 = 32$ different actual sentences.

## Using the Pattern for Speaking Practice

Read off the first sentence, *les rues sont larges*, several times until you can do so without having to read each word. Then cover up the first part of the pattern (*les rues sont . . .*) and, looking only at the adjectives, continue to say *les rues sont étroites, les rues sont grandes* and *les rues sont petites*. When you can do this successfully you will find that the first part (subject and verb) presents no difficulty, and you can then either switch to the negative form (*les rues ne sont pas larges, . . . pas étroites*, etc.) or introduce another of the subjects (*les maisons sont larges, sont étroites*, etc.). When you consider that you have got the feel of the whole pattern, which may be before you have actually spoken thirty-two sentences, cover up the material and write down half a dozen assorted statements that you can make from memory out of the stock. You thus get in some spelling practice, which you can readily check by reference to the original, and to make sure that you have remained aware of their meanings say them in English. If you can do so without hesitation write their English translation down for use later; if not, go back to each word to remind yourself of its meaning and try the sentences again.

Then construct another pattern with some further elements and repeat the process. At the end of the time which you have allotted yourself for one period of study turn to the English sentences that you wrote as the result of practice with the first batch of material and try to say each one immediately in French without looking at the original.

By simply "doing" the exercises as set out in the textbook you will have had practice only in translation; by adopting the above method however you will in one lesson have practised speaking freely, writing, reading, interpreting and translating.

## EXPANDING THE PATTERN AND SELECTING MATERIAL

One of the purposes of arranging sentence patterns is to increase the number of practicable examples. Often it will be found that a textbook devotes half a dozen pages in each chapter to grammatical theory and then, as an afterthought, little more than half a page to exercises based on it. Even if there are as few as ten sentence examples in the foreign language, however, it may be objected that too much time would be lost in expanding each one into a pattern for practice as described above. Yet this is in fact unnecessary, since one pattern will generally be found to cover the majority of sentences given in the exercise. For example, the exercise from which the above pattern was taken consists of eighteen sentences, of which nine fit into it, and since the remainder represent between them just two other types of sentence it becomes necessary only to set out three patterns to cover the exercise material. Each pattern, as we have already illustrated, is extremely versatile and is capable of producing many more working examples than will in most cases be required. At a rough estimate, this method may easily increase the exercise material tenfold, so that our previous eighteen sentences could be used to produce one hundred and eighty.

In expanding the pattern so as to give as many different sentences as possible there is one particular danger to be avoided, and that is to overlook the fact that change in one element may affect the rest of the sentence. For example, while it is possible to say in French *Les rues sont petites, les maisons, les villes et les voitures sont petites*, it is *not* possible to describe *les châteaux* by the same form of the adjective. *Petites* is the feminine plural form of *petit*, being put in this form to agree with *rues*, *maisons*, *villes* and *voitures*, all of which are feminine nouns. *Les châteaux* is a masculine plural noun, and as such its inclusion in the list of nouns forming the first element of the pattern will necessitate the change of *petites* to *petits*, with a difference in pronunciation.

To illustrate this feature we shall take the following vocabulary—

| | | | |
|---|---|---|---|
| l'homme: | man | grand (fem. grande): | big |
| le garçon: | boy | petit (fem. petite): | small |
| le facteur: | postman | gros (fem. grosse): | stout, fat |
| la femme: | woman | est: | is |
| la fillette: | girl | n'est pas: | is not |
| l'actrice: | actress | devient: | is growing or becoming |

and arrange it as follows to ensure that the masculine form of the adjective will apply to masculine nouns, and the feminine form to feminine nouns—

| | | |
|---|---|---|
| l'homme<br>le garçon<br>le facteur | est | grand<br>petit<br>gros |
| | n'est pas | |
| la femme<br>la fillette<br>l'actrice | devient | grande<br>petite<br>grosse |

This type of distinction arises in many sentence patterns, and it is therefore essential to follow the grammar section closely and read through the sentences in the exercise of each chapter before constructing such a pattern. The feature is one which is easily incorporated by the device shown above. To summarize, it may be stated that elements of a sentence which affect or must agree with others should be placed on the same level and separated by a horizontal line. (In the above illustration the verb element, *est/n'est pas/devient*, is not affected by the distinction between masculine and feminine, thus it need not be split up but can be spread out to show that it applies to all subjects.)

Once fluency in the use of masculine and feminine forms has been acquired it is good practice to join two short sentences into one composite sentence to contrast masculine and feminine forms. So, with the addition of *et = and*, one might say *L'homme est grand et la femme est grande, le garçon est petit et la fillette est petite*, etc.

The first difficulties confronting a learner of German are those of gender and case: nouns may be masculine, feminine or neuter, and according to their function in any given sentence may be nominative, accusative, genitive or dative; any of these factors will tend to affect the form of the noun and will definitely affect the form of the article that goes with it. The first chapter of a German textbook might consist of the following—

> GRAMMAR: The Definite Article preceding masculine nouns is *der* in the Nominative Case, i.e. when the noun is the subject of a verb, and *den* when it is in the Accusative Case, i.e. the direct object of a verb, e.g. *Der Mann sieht den Mann:* the man sees the man. The first man is the (nominative) subject, the second is the (accusative) object. Nouns in German are written with an initial capital letter.

> VOCABULARY: 
>
> | | | | |
> |---|---|---|---|
> | der Mann: | man | sieht: | sees |
> | der Sohn: | son | hört: | hears |
> | der Hund: | dog | sucht: | looks for, seeks |
> | der Vogel: | bird | findet: | finds. |

From this material the following pattern can be formed—

| Der | Mann<br>Sohn<br>Hund<br>Vogel | sieht<br>hört<br>sucht<br>findet | den | Vogel<br>Hund<br>Sohn<br>Mann |
|---|---|---|---|---|

Five or ten minutes spoken practice with some of the sixty-four available sentences will result in a ready command of the nominative and accusative cases of masculine nouns.

Often much labour is put into descriptive grammar which leads only to unnecessary complications. In this case, for example, many textbooks would set out the cases of all three genders in the following tabular form—

| | Masc. | Fem. | Neut. |
|---|---|---|---|
| Nominative | der | die | das |
| Accusative | den | die | das |

Ignoring the trees and looking at the wood for a moment you will find that this tells you quite simply that there is no special accusative form for feminine and neuter nouns, so that there is no need to spend time on two more patterns similar to that for masculine nouns. Instead the next step is to construct a pattern that plunges you immediately into all three genders.

VOCABULARY:  die Frau:       woman
              die Katze:      cat
              das Mädchen:    girl (note that this word is
                              grammatically neuter)
              das Pferd:      horse

| | | | |
|---|---|---|---|
| Der    Mann<br>        Hund | sieht | den    Hund<br>        Mann | |
| Die    Frau<br>        Katze | hört<br>sucht | die    Katze<br>        Frau | |
| Das    Mädchen<br>        Pferd | findet | das    Pferd<br>        Mädchen | |

The sample sentences so far produced in French and German
have been similar in pattern to their English equivalents. Thus
*La maison est petite* corresponds word for word with *The house is
small*, and *Der Mann sieht den Hund* with *The man sees the dog*. The
advantages of learning through constant speech practice become
more apparent when there are differences between the English and
the foreign language pattern. In languages close to English the
basic sentence types tend to be very similar in pattern, and it is
not until the later stages that differences are noticeable.

Swedish, however, presents one peculiarity which affects the
feel of the sentence from the very beginning, and that is the use of
an **enclitic** (or suffixed) definite article. The first steps in a Swedish
course might well introduce the following material—

GRAMMAR: Nouns are classified either as Common (associated
with the sound -**n**) or as Neuter (associated with the sound -**t**). The
Indefinite Article is either **en** or **ett** according to gender, and the Definite
is formed by suffixing either -**en** or -**et** to the noun concerned.

VOCABULARY:  en häst:      a horse        hästen:     the horse
              en flicka:    a girl         flickan:    the girl
              en person:    a person       personen:   the person
              ett djur:     an animal      djuret:     the animal
              ett möss:     a mouse        mösset:     the mouse
              ett barn:     a child        barnet:     the child
              är:           is             är inte:    is not

Form from this a pattern for speech drill—

| Hästen Flickan Personen | är | en | person flicka häst |
|---|---|---|---|
| Djuret Mösset Barnet | är inte | ett | barn möss djur |

This pattern provides sufficient material to introduce painlessly the use of the enclitic definite article and to contrast it at the same time with the indefinite. Not all of the sentences obtainable direct from the above pattern would necessarily make rational sense (though all would be grammatically correct), but this is not necessarily a bad thing. In the first place you should notice as soon as you speak or read a sentence whether or not it is nonsensical, and if in fact an irrational statement such as *Flicken är ett djur* does strike you as odd then you can be sure that you are aware of the meaning, which is the first step to thinking in the second language. In the second place you would at a later stage introduce questions in the language to which the above statements are answers, so that you might ask *Är flicken ett djur?* and reply *Nej, flickan är inte ett djur.*

We noticed in German that it became unnecessary to practise separately the accusative forms *die* and *das* because they were the same as the nominative and so presented no new difficulty. Similarly you may notice in the Swedish examples that there has been no necessity to learn as an irregularity or separate statement of fact "the definite article ending -**en** drops the **e** when preceded by a vowel, e.g. *flicka* becomes *flickan*, and not *flickaen*." This change, which is quite straightforward and could almost be anticipated, is automatically incorporated into the pattern and automatically learnt through usage.

Differences of sentence pattern are even more obvious in the case of Welsh and other Celtic languages, in that the verb is placed at the beginning of the sentence in most cases and is followed by its subject, a feature which does not normally occur in Germanic or Romance languages. A typical Welsh sentence from the first chapter of a textbook may serve as a model—

Welsh: Mae'r bws yn aros ar y stryd.
Word-for-word: Is the bus in stopping on the street.
English: The bus stops (*or* is stopping) in the street.

Many other sentences based on this pattern can be constructed by changing the elements as follows: the subject *bws* can be changed, using vocabulary from the same chapter, to *car*, *tad* (father), *plismon* (policeman), *bachgen* (boy); the main verb *yn aros* (stopping) to *mynd* (going), *cerdded* (walking), *rhedeg* (running); and the adverbial phrase *ar y stryd* to *yn y sgwar* (in the square), *i'r dref* (to the town), *i'r parc* (to the park).

When you look ahead to the last exercise or so in a textbook on a language which you are only just beginning, you wonder whether you will ever manage to find your way around such long, apparently complicated sentences as *Many of the buildings in various quarters of New York are extremely high; typewriters are very useful, especially nowadays when many people write in an almost illegible manner; the coffee-tree is a tree the colour of whose fruit changes from green to red;* (all of which come from Exercise 27 of *Teach Yourself Spanish*). Yet when you have progressed that far you will realize at a glance that the apparently greater complexity is usually quantitative rather than qualitative: the basic sentence patterns are the same as those you will have learnt in the first few lessons, and it is only the length of each element that has been increased. For example, the above three sentences have at their core the following simple phrases: *Buildings are high; typewriters are useful; the coffee-tree is a tree;* which are not different in kind from our previous elementary sentences *the streets are wide; the horse is an animal,* and so on. By this stage it will not be necessary to keep on constructing patterns as such, for if the "feel" of each type of sentence has been satisfactorily acquired and a fair amount of vocabulary learnt you should find that you will be able to produce other lengthy sentences at sight based on the model of anyone given in the exercise.

Using material that has been introduced before the exercise in which the last mentioned sentence for translation into Spanish, the correct version—*El cafeto es una planta, el color de cuyos frutos se cambia de verde en colorado* suggests other sentences such as—

*Es un hombre, el color de cuyos ojos se cambia de verde en azul* (he is a man whose eyes change in colour from green to blue), and so on. As a general rule it is always desirable to find more than one sample sentence of a particular pattern illustrating usage of the same grammatical point, for the more that can be found and practised the more chances you have of retaining in your memory not just a particular collection of words forming one particular sentence but the grammatical structure behind it that will enable you to produce many other statements like it as the occasion demands. In the early stages this is achieved by means of the formalized pattern as illustrated in this chapter, but later on you should find no difficulty in producing variations on any given theme.

# CHAPTER 8

# USE OF TEXTBOOK—QUESTION
# AND ANSWER METHOD

WE have seen that it is better to learn words and phrases as components of complete sentences than it is to learn them and grammatical rules in isolation, since for the most part communication is only achieved by means of complete sentences and the words and phrases do not normally occur in isolation. The sentence pattern method effectively achieves this end, but even so it does not completely solve the problems of learning a language, especially alone. For it is not sufficient merely to state that the purpose of language is to communicate, implying the communication of statements of fact from one person to another: even bees can do just that. It would be more accurate to say that the function of speech is to *converse*, implying a two-way communication *between* people. As such it will be realized that even complete sentences do not, for the most part, themselves occur in isolation, but are the responses to stimuli provided in conversation as the result of question and answer, supposition and conclusion, opinion and discussion.

The clearest form of stimulus and response in language is that of question and answer. The only way to get a reticent person to talk is to ask him questions. Ask polite questions of a stranger in a pub and you are likely to get into conversation; make statements and you are more likely to get into an argument. In a court of law, where a witness is legally bound not only to speak, but moreover to speak the truth, it is linguistically possible for counsel to frame questions that will elicit the exact type of answer he requires, however unwilling the witness may be. In short it is true to say that any statement may be regarded as the answer to at least one question, and can occur as at least one response to the stimulus of any particular question.

As a lone language learner the nearest you can get to oral practice at conversational speed is to ask yourself questions based on the patterns you are doing at any given time and to produce some of the sample sentences which you have made available as the answers to those questions. This method may appear odd at first sight, but it can be shown to be both practicable and desirable. It is desirable for two main reasons: firstly, many who travel abroad for the first time often find that they need to use their newly acquired language more for asking questions than for making statements, although this aspect has generally been left insufficiently practised in school or classes since, especially under the Indirect Method, it is usually the teacher who asks the questions and the pupil who provides the anwers; and secondly because by keeping up a series of questions and answers based on the same material, which is easy to do after a little practice, it is possible to attain conversational speed and a close approximation to genuine speech situations, resulting in quicker and more automatic responses encouraging an ability to "think in the foreign language." It is quite a practical method since in most cases the number of interrogatives (words introducing questions) in any language is quite small—basically fewer than ten—and they occur within the first few chapters of the textbook.

The basic interrogatives which should be learnt early on are as follows (given in three major languages)—

| | ENGLISH | FRENCH | GERMAN |
|---|---|---|---|
| 1. | Who? | Qui? | Wer? |
| 2. | What? | Qu'est-ce qui? | Was? |
| 3. | What . . . like? | Comment? | Wie? |
| 4. | Which? | Quel(le)? | Welch-? |
| 5. | Where? | Où? | Wo? |
| 6. | When? | Quand? | Wann? |
| 7. | How? | Comment? | Wie? |
| 8. | How much, many? | Combien? | Wieviel? |
| 9. | Why? | Pourquoi? | Warum? |

It will be noted that on the whole each interrogative requires as the main part of its answer a particular part of speech, e.g. *who* and *what* will be answered by nouns or pronouns, *which* by demonstrative words (e.g. which door?—*that* one), *when* by adverbs of time, and so on. (Incidentally, *what . . . like?* listed above in the first column, is the peculiarly awkward way of asking for a description of something in English, the main part of the answer being an adjective. In most languages this is expressed in a less roundabout way:

English: What's her mother like?—She's very kind.
French: Comment est sa mère?—Elle est très gentille.
German: Wie ist ihre Mutter?—Sie ist sehr gütig.

Be warned, however, when first learning an interrogative word, always to find in the textbook an example of its usage before framing any questions and answers.

In addition to the above interrogatives many languages have set expressions which serve to turn a complete statement into a question requiring the answer *yes* or *no*, e.g. French *N'est-ce pas?*, German *Nicht wahr?*, Spanish *¿No es verdad?*, Swedish *Eller hur?* English does not have such an expression, the verb is repeated instead, e.g., *He came, didn't he? You are, aren't you?* Similarly it should be noted that some languages do not have an equivalent for *yes* and *no* as the answer, but repeat the verb, e.g., Welsh says *Did he come?—He came* (= yes); *Are you?—I'm not* (= no).

In the early stages, of course, there are very few questions to which sentences from textbook translation exercises lend themselves, but here the main value lies in constant spoken repetition of similar phrases. Referring to our previous pattern in Swedish for example—

| | | | |
|---|---|---|---|
| Hästen Flickan | är | en | person flicka |
| Personen | | | häst |
| Djuret | är inte | ett | barn |
| Mösset Barnet | | | möss djur |

the following series of questions and answers might arise—

Är flickan en person? Ja, flickan är en person.
Är hästen en person? Nej, hästen är inte en person, det är ett djur.
Barnet är inte ett djur, eller hur? Nej, det är en person.
Ett möss är ett djur, eller hur? Ja, det är ett djur.

(Translation—
Is the girl a person? Yes, the girl is a person.
Is the horse a person? No, the horse isn't a person, it is an animal.
The child isn't an animal, is it? No, it is a person.
A mouse is an animal, isn't it? Yes, it is an animal.)

Later on, when reading passages are encountered, more scope will be provided for particular interrogatives. The following sentences come from the beginning of a reading section from *Teach Yourself French*—

*Tout le monde sait très bien que Londres est la plus grande ville de l'Europe. Paris est loin d'être aussi grand que la capitale de l'Angleterre.* (Everyone knows very well that London is the biggest city in Europe. Paris is far from being as large as the capital of England.)

Some questions that can be formed from the above include—
Où est Londres? Où est l'Angleterre? Où est Paris? Comment est Londres? Londres est plus grand que Paris, n'est-ce pas? Quelle est la capitale de la France? Qui sait que Londres est la plus grande ville de l'Europe? Paris est une ville de l'Europe, n'est-ce pas?—and so on.

Finally it should become possible with greater command of the language to get away from answers contained in the passage; often a single word will be found to start off a "thought association test." For example, mention of the word *Bäcker* (= baker) in German might give rise to—

| | |
|---|---|
| Was ist ein Bäcker? | What is a baker? |
| Ein Mann, der Brot macht. | A man who makes bread. |
| Wo arbeitet er? | Where does he work? |
| In einer Bäckerei. | In a bakery. |
| Und wer kauft das Brot? | And who buys the bread? |
| Jedermann kauft es. | Everyone buys it. |
| Warum kaufen wir Brot? | Why do we buy bread? |
| Um zu essen. | To eat. |
| Wieviel kostet es? | How much is it? |
| (Und so weiter) | (And so on) |

# CHAPTER 9

# USE OF PERIODICALS

As we saw in the survey of materials in Chapter 6 the value of periodicals in the language you are learning lies in the presentation of continuous text on subjects of interest: the written language is presented "live" and you become acquainted with its constructions through becoming involved with the matter communicated, which makes a necessary change from the textbook situation of deliberate study on isolated points.

The questions "what sort of text to look for?" and "how to make use of the text?" are bound together, and may best be answered by considering the possible immediate aims of using continuous text. Two stand out—

1. To meet new constructions and vocabulary and to practise them both orally and in writing, i.e. actively to learn new material.

2. To become better acquainted with the flow and stylistic usage of the language, i.e. to increase an intuitive feeling for it as an aid to the general requirement of "thinking in the language."

The choice of text and of approach may be made in accordance with these aims.

## Active Learning

Active learning involves conscious practice, and, as suggested previously, the Sentence Pattern and Question and Answer methods enable this to be achieved effectively through spoken practice. The text should, therefore, be descriptive rather than narrative, in straightforward, even rather colloquial style rather than literary, with a tendency to shorter sentences and much use of the present tense (or equivalent). In newspapers the emphasis should be on features, rather than news items, dealing with clearly defined subjects. As an aid to comprehension it is handy to select articles on subjects with which you are quite well acquainted, or even, if possible, to find an elementary textbook in that language on a subject in which you are particularly interested. In this way you will find it possible to acquire a larger amount of vocabulary, since many languages derive their specialized and technical terms from the same roots.

New constructions may be learnt orally by taking the sentence in which a construction occurs and treating it as the basis of a new pattern following the principles suggested in Chapter 7. The pattern can be expanded by the substitution of both already known vocabulary which it may be desirable to revise, and new words taken from the article so that they too may be learnt—remembering that vocabulary is better learnt in context and usage than in the abstract from lists of isolated words.

The Question and Answer method may be followed in several ways. For example, you might select a short sentence or sentences at random, treat them as answers to questions, and ask the questions which they imply. The same may be done in respect of captions to photographs or drawings illustrating the text. Or you may imagine that you are being asked to define any new term or word that may occur: ask the meaning of it, and give the answer as far as possible in one short but complete sentence. This provides practical revision of construction and vocabulary that have already been learnt, or may allow further practice of new material. If you use a tape-recorder, record the questions (leaving between them suitable gaps for the provision of answers), and then give the answers as revision material in your next study session.

To consolidate what you have been learning through spoken practice turn next to the written word—

1. Write down at random any of the sentences which may have occurred as the result of the Sentence Pattern construction—try to produce at least a dozen.

2. Compose your own captions to any illustrations that may appear, or expand those already given. If there is a scenic photograph, describe what you see in it—in a static scene you would of course concentrate on suitable adjectives, and in a scene of activity on verbs.

3. Using complete sentences, write definitions of new elements of vocabulary that have been learnt.

4. Using simple sentences and avoiding too much detail, write a résumé of the article.

5. Finally check everything you have written—sentences from the pattern you have constructed, captions from any already given, and as much material as possible from the original text. Concentrate on the mistakes you have made, even if only slips of the pen in spelling, by rewriting completely any sentence in which a mistake occurs.

### BACKGROUND CONTACT

Any article you read and study will increase your background knowledge of the language: it soaks you in a new sort of linguistic atmosphere and surroundings. If you are receptive to this atmosphere you may develop a greater feeling for the language, enabling you unconsciously to select vocabulary most appropriate for a given context and to arrange the elements of your sentences in a more authentic way. This is the basis of that indefinable term "style," and one proof of receptivity to the character of a language is an increasing ability to distinguish between the styles of writing which you may encounter, the colloquial as opposed to the literary construction, the startling, emotive and subjective as opposed to the subtle, logical and objective choice of words.

You cannot make yourself naturally more receptive to such points, but it is possible to work in such a way that your own degree of receptiveness may be used to best advantage and may, therefore, with constant practice be improved.

Here it is better to select articles written in a more literary style: they may include for example short stories, historical features, articles filling in the background of current events, biographical features and so on. Longer sentences, a richer vocabulary, and greater use of past tenses will be characteristic of such items. Amongst methods of using text of this type we may mention—

1. Reading and re-reading aloud complete paragraphs, concentrating first on getting the actual sounds and words to flow smoothly without stumbling, and then on giving each phrase and sentence its due emphasis and tone of voice according to its place in the context.

2. Rewriting the article or some passages from it in a more direct style, using shorter sentences and simpler vocabulary, or, as before, doing this as a résumé or précis.

3. Translating passages into English and then, at a later date, translating from your English back into the original language.

4. As either a written or a spoken exercise, for any type of text, choose a passage which uses one tense exclusively and reproduce it with a change of tense, for example if it is in the past, change to the present or the future, if in the present, to the past or the future.

# CHAPTER 10

# USE OF RECORDS AND TAPE

RECORD-PLAYERS and tape-recorders are obviously of great value to the language learner since both deal primarily with live speech. There, however, the resemblance ends. Records constitute a main course and aim to be complete in themselves, although a certain amount of written text is indispensable to their method, while at present tape is only an accompaniment: for the private learner, outside the language laboratory, it comes into its own only in conjunction with records or when a native speaker is available for personal co-operation.

## RECORD COURSES

The idea behind recorded language courses is that you learn to speak a foreign language the natural way, by listening to native speakers reading graded passages of prose and dialogue at normal speed and in natural context. You can follow the text in an accompanying book and then read it for yourself out loud; generally the text consists of description/narration, dialogue, and question/answer, so that you may have practice in all types of speech situation. Great use is made in the course-book of labelled pictures and scene-setting illustrations so that to a large extent the process of translation is by-passed in favour of direct association of foreign sounds with recognizable visual images.

The essential feature of a language record is the provision of live speech by a native speaker: to what extent is this a practical advantage?

Firstly, it is not entirely true to state that you learn to speak by listening—in fact, you learn by listening and then *imitating*. Accurate imitation cannot be effected at great length. Even one side of a 10-in. 78 rpm record provides a large amount of material to be remembered—about three minutes—and several hearings will be necessary before you can attempt the passage with confidence. The advantage here is held by those records which alternate short sections of speech with gaps for your imitation of them. Even so, the value of this procedure cannot be fully realized since you have no way of checking the accuracy of your results (although here a tape-recorder is extremely useful, as will be shown). It is true that you will have had practice in speaking whole sentences, but this is no different from the result achieved by the sentence-pattern method of textbooks (Chapter 7).

Secondly, the provision of live speech by a native speaker suggests practice in following and understanding the spoken word. The value of this procedure is lessened if at the same time you are reading the text printed in the book. Ideally therefore you should make yourself acquainted with the vocabulary and essential grammatical features of the passage beforehand, then close your eyes and see how much of the record you can actually follow with sufficient comprehension. Of course this will not be necessary where the relevant section of the accompanying book consists of illustration (labelled or otherwise) and no text: in fact this procedure is more helpful than the actual script.

The main danger of a record course is its tendency to encourage, if you are not careful, a state of passivity: listening, reading, following may easily take the place of verbal activity, with unsatisfactory results.

### Choosing a Record Course

Most record libraries stock one or more of the better known courses; if you belong to such a library you will find that this has two distinct advantages. The main advantage is financial, since the personal acquisition of a complete set in any language series is one of the most expensive ways of learning another language, though not necessarily more effective for that. The second is that you can judge the relative merits of each if you do intend to buy a set later; and of course you can get more variety in your work by using all the different makes available. If you have not access to many different makes the first step is to write for descriptive literature from each one and base your choice upon the method described and the sample extracts from accompanying textbooks. The following series are available in Britain—

ASSiMiL, Godalming, Surrey.

Daily Express Language Series, Fleet Street, London, E.C.4.

Linguaphone, The Linguaphone Institute Ltd., Linguaphone House, 207–209 Regent Street, London, W.1.

P.I.L.L. (Programmed Instruction Language Learning), The World of Learning Ltd., Richmond, Surrey.

Rainbow "Instant" Language Series, Keith Prowse & Co. (Wholesale Div.), 202 Tooting High Street, London, S.W.17.

In 1965 there were nearly a dozen such courses on the market in this country; some have since ceased to advertise, and may no longer be available.

Most companies will allow you several days' free trial if you ask, or will invite you to visit showrooms for a demonstration. When trying the records out the following points should be taken into consideration—

1. Records and acompanying textbook should be easy to use in conjunction with each other and not involve complicated instructions.

2. Textbooks should, by preference, be written in appropriate script and/or the International Phonetic Alphabet (*see* Chapter 11).

3. Instructions for learning should adequately encourage active participation on your part.

4. Recorded speech should be in complete sentences and on everyday topics.

## Tape

At time of writing the only ready prepared language tapes are merely taped versions of some of the records available in the series mentioned above. The taped language drills of the sort that are readily available from several different firms for use in language laboratories are generally too expensive for the private student. Such tapes, which necessarily run two tracks, one for question (or stimulus) which remains fixed, and the other for answer (or response) which is continuously used, erased and re-used by the learner, would render the tape-recorder a far more effective medium for home language learners than the gramophone. As it is, tape is only of use where you have some access to speech in the foreign language by a native, whether in person or on record. Its principal advantage lies in the possibility of immediate comparison of your own speech with that of a native, and in that it enables you to judge objectively your own progress.

If you have a tape-recorder with variable speeds remember that always the higher the speed, the greater the fidelity. For the general purpose of practising speech patterns the lower speeds, $3\frac{3}{4}$ and $1\frac{7}{8}$ inches per second, will prove adequate, but for oral exercises concerned with accent and pronunciation the higher speeds, $7\frac{1}{2}$ and 15 ips, are preferable. If you have a two- (or more-) track recorder, record the stimuli (i.e. questions requiring an answer, or sentences requiring translation, etc.) beforehand on one track, then remain on the other for your responses, erasing them and giving them again without affecting the stimulus track. This method is not, however, immediately practicable at home unless (*a*) you can get an experienced teacher to prepare and record the stimuli for you, or (*b*) you are learning one of the major languages for which you may buy ready-prepared exercises in book form.

## TAPE WITH RECORDS

A tape-recorder is a valuable adjunct to a gramophone and language records, particularly as far as pronunciation is concerned. Exactly how best use is to be made of it depends on the nature of the record.

If the record contains "gaps" in which you are to answer questions or repeat words and sentences the easiest method is to record the questions and your responses as a whole, then to play back and compare your pronunciation with that of the original speaker. You should try also to judge the speed and accuracy with which you have made the responses, noting points to be improved before recording the process again. If the material consists of straight-forward question and answer in the foreign language, the result should sound like an easy and natural conversation. This is a little more difficult than it sounds, requiring as much practice as is necessary to induce confidence on your part: you should aim at giving your answers as if you are imparting vital information, speaking fairly slowly, loudly and clearly.

The record may consist simply of the reading of a piece of text, in which case all you can do without too much trouble is to record your version afterwards, then play the record again, followed by your own reading, and keep doing so until you feel that your result sounds as authentic as the original.

## OTHER USES OF TAPE

If you have a native speaker of the language you are learning available to help you, you will naturally find many ways of using a tape recorder, depending on the extent to which you may expect to receive assistance. One way in which it might be of particular value is in helping to overcome the difficulties of linguistic shyness in the presence of a speaker, especially in the early stages: you may feel that you have a better accent and greater fluency in reading when by yourself, in which case you may record your solo turns and play them back afterwards for criticism and advice.

If you have no records, and no native speaker, and are therefore using a tape-recorder solely as an addition to learning from books, the proper role of the recorder is to act as a second person by means of taped questions which you have previously prepared yourself. These may be of two sorts; in both cases it is essential when preparing the tape to remember to leave a sufficiently large gap between the questions for producing the response live.

One method is to record a series of phrases and sentences in English based on sentence patterns of the type described in Chapter 7, which will give you practice in speedy interpretation. The value of this will, of course, lessen as you become more used to the script and so such exercises need to be changed frequently to avoid the staleness of parrot-like repetition. The other is to record questions in the foreign language (*see* Chapter 8) and to answer these live as quickly and fluently as possible. Staleness can be more easily avoided by this method, as it is possible to record a series of questions whose answers may vary from time to time. It is good warming-up practice at the beginning of each learning session to play and answer a tape which asks you the date, the time, the weather, when you got up in the morning, what you had to eat, and so on.

Finally, and for the sake of completeness, it will be found useful in the more advanced stages to tape wireless programmes in the foreign language from their country of origin. Since the broadcasts are intended for native speakers you will generally find the speech too fast and indistinct in detail to follow successfully at first hearing, but as you play them back phrases and sentences will begin to stand out intelligibly, and will provide you with an opportunity to practise faster speech with the correct rhythm and intonation of the original.

# CHAPTER 11

# USE OF PHONETICS

This chapter is about pronunciation and the acquisition of a correct accent in the language you are learning, hence it is mainly concerned with learning to *speak* the foreign language. "Phonetics" is a general term for a method of writing a language in such a way that the exact sounds are shown in relation to one another. To this extent we are also concerned with a version of the *written* language, but not of its usual orthography.

The reason for the discrepancy between the usual alphabet and a phonetic one arises from the basic problem of representing sounds by visual symbols, which is well exemplified in the case of English. The Roman alphabet, in which English and most other western European languages are written, consists of 20 basic characters, subsequent borrowings and variations bringing the total to the 26 used in English.* Since English contains at least 40 different phonemes or distinct sounds, and most of the others over 30, it happens that some symbols are used to represent more than one sound—thus, for example, the symbol **a** has different values in the words *lad, lard, wad, wall, wade, ware, woman.* At the same time, since spelling follows conventional rules and traditional patterns it tends to remain fixed, especially where there is a strong literary tradition, while the actual spoken language standard changes imperceptibly with each generation that speaks it. Thus we have spellings which no longer correspond to the modern pronunciation, and many cases in which the same sound is written in many different ways, e.g. that represented usually by **ee** as in *bee* is also heard in *be, beat, believe, receive, key, quay, machine*; and other instances have arisen of different values for one symbol, e.g. the **s** of *house, hose, sure, leisure.* In this respect French is as awkward as English, if not worse. Even languages which tend to be "phonetically" written, that is, retain fairly constant values for particular symbols, such as Welsh, need the use of "digraphs" (combinations of letters) for distinct sounds, e.g. (in Welsh) **ch, dd, ff, ll, ng, ph, rh, si, th.**

The aim of a phonetic alphabet is to have one symbol corresponding with one sound, and one sound represented by the same symbol,

---

* Icelandic adds ð and þ for the sounds represented by **th** in modern English, but most other languages of Europe using the Roman alphabet extend it by the use of accents—thus, for example, é, è, ê in French are three different letters and represent three different sounds, though not consistently.

that by means of so a key describing each sound and symbol exactly any passage of text may be read correctly and a good pronunciation acquired through constant practice. To what extent this aim can be achieved is a question to be discussed later in this chapter.

## ACCENT AND PRONUNCIATION

We can often guess the native language of a foreigner who speaks English with a non-English accent, and occasionally identify foreign speech by means of the accent even if we are incapable of understanding or distinguishing any of the words. We are not usually conscious of the individual features which make up a particular accent: we recognize it intuitively by its general aura of identity, in much the same way as we might recognize a friend from a distance by the way he walks, stands, or carries an umbrella. At this level of awareness we could call a particular accent the personality of a particular language.

At a more analytic level, the accent of a language comprises three main features—

    1. The individual sounds of which it is composed (**pronunciation**)

    2. The speed and intensity with which syllables are run together, or separated, or contrasted (**rhythm**)

    3. Variation in pitch—the pattern of rise and fall of the voice over phrases and sentences (**intonation**)

The fact that each language has its own accent distinct from that of any other indicates that the human speech organs are physically capable of producing countless variations of sound, stress and intonation, so that in theory anybody could speak any language with no natural difficulties of pronunciation. This is however invalidated in practice because the use by one person of the accent of his mother language becomes a deeply ingrained habit which has to be broken in order to learn another: basically it is the habitual rather than the physical aspect that causes difficulty. The difficulty is increased by two further factors: first, that in speaking a foreign language some muscles used for speech are brought greatly into play to produce in that language a sound which does not exist in the mother tongue, so that they have never become fully efficient and at first only operate with concentration and effort; and second, that there may be defects in sound *perception*, varying from individual to individual—that is that a person may not be able to produce a particular foreign sound because his ear is incapable of distinguishing any difference between it and its nearest equivalent in his own language. However, complete inability to distinguish any difference between foreign and known sounds is probably rarer than tone-deafness or colour-blindness.

If you are unfortunate enough to lack this ability it will not stop you from making yourself understood in the foreign language; but if, as is more likely, you can make yourself aware of the nature of foreign sounds it is desirable for your own satisfaction and for the comfort of foreigners to learn the correct accent. A foreign accent, as yours would be abroad, sounds quaint at first, but soon palls.

How is a satisfactory accent then to be acquired? Theoretically, the answer is simple. The best way is to put yourself as much as possible in contact with living speech—hold as much conversation with native speakers as circumstances allow; the second best way is to listen to and imitate as much recorded speech as may be available on record, tape or film. In both cases, assuming that the practical difficulties are overcome and that you have access to either (this becomes an initiative test, but *see* page 40), you have still to remember that imitation is an active process: firstly, when you are listening, you must make yourself conscious of the total flow of speech (this is more important and in any case easier than trying to concentrate on individual sounds)—the rise and fall of the voice and the placing of stress and emphasis; secondly, when you are speaking, try to act the part of a native, to the extent of imitating gestures and facial expressions. In the long run you will find that, if you can successfully mimic and faithfully impersonate a native speaker, a correct reproduction of the intonation and gestures will tend automatically to bring out the authentic individual sounds of the language. In that case slight differences between the genuine sounds and the nearest English equivalents will be less noticeable. The difference in pronunciation between the English sounds **p, t, k** (or hard **c**) and those of French is very slight, but providing the intonation is good it can be ignored. If you speak French with a good intonation, your use of the English sounds **p, t, k** will pass unnoticed, but if, on the other hand, you go to great pains to adopt the French **p, t, k** sounds and still speak with the intonation and mannerisms of an English person, you will simply sound foreign.

Since you cannot concentrate on intonation until you have sufficient grasp of the language to enable you to hold a simple conversation, it follows that a good grounding in the construction of the language is necessary before you can turn to the business of acquiring a genuine accent. In other words, if you do not have access to live or recorded speech from the outset, do not spend a lot of time on trying to pick up a good accent from books—it is impossible. Two things are possible, however.  First, a general idea of individual sounds can be achieved by means of a written description, and a phonetic alphabet can be of use in the initial stages—we shall come on to that immediately.  Second, it is possible to speak the foreign language intelligibly at first and then, at a later stage, when your knowledge of the language is greater and favourable circumstances obtain, to acquire a good accent.

## The International Phonetic Alphabet (I.P.A.)— and Others

Your foreign language textbook will probably begin with an introduction to the sounds of the language, or give this and reading passages for practice in the first chapter.  This will be in one of several forms according to the orthography of the language concerned.

1. If the language makes use of some alphabet other than the Roman (others used in Europe are Greek and Cyrillic)* then, whether the orthography is regular and consistent or otherwise, a chapter devoted to reading and writing is essential and should be mastered before any grammatical work is attempted.

2. If diacritical marks (accents) are used, it is important to understand when, where, and why they appear, since their omission or misuse may well give rise to ambiguities, while in many cases their appearance is an aid to pronunciation.

3. If the language is written "phonetically," i.e. with consistent correspondence between sounds and individual symbols, and if, at the same time, most of the sounds are very similar to their English counterparts, the author may make use either of "imitated pronunciation" or of a phonetic system of his own which is only applicable to that particular language.

4. If the language has an inconsistent orthography, such as English and French have, or if the sounds are in many cases considerably different from any English counterparts, then, if any phonetic system is to be used at all, it should be the I.P.A. (*see* heading above).

We have seen that a good accent involves more than the correct enunciation of individual sounds, that it is a question of intonation and speech mannerisms.  The latter cannot be very well represented

* An acquaintance with the Gothic script in which German is still to be found in print is not essential: it is dropping out of favour and if necessary can easily be picked up.  It is therefore not worth using a textbook for German printed in this style.

on paper, hence a good accent cannot be learnt from books. A start can be made however if a reasonable description of individual sounds is available in your textbook, and this is one point to look for, regardless of any phonetic alphabet that may be used. The description of each sound can generally be achieved quite well if the nearest English equivalent is given as a starting point, and an intelligible method of changing the position of certain speech organs is presented (*see* Fig. 2). If you feel confident that you are

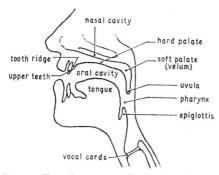

FIG. 2. THE PRINCIPAL ORGANS OF SPEECH

producing a fair approximation of the correct sound—examples should include words in which the sound occurs in different positions—then try to keep to it every time you come across the appropriate symbols. If you are producing something that is certainly different from English, but which you are not confident is the correct foreign sound, then do not waste time learning a possible mispronunciation—better to fall back on the nearest English equivalent until you have an opportunity to hear the spoken language.

If the author uses a phonetic system, for example the usual Roman alphabet as used in English but with the addition of certain variations on some symbols or some accents, make sure you follow carefully the description given of each sound. Such a system is mostly inferior to the I.P.A. for reasons which will be given, but is certainly preferable to "imitated pronunciation." Imitated pronunciation is simply the device of writing in the foreign language following the regularities of English orthography, e.g. since the sound represented by **i** in *machine* is usually written **ee,** and the **ch** of the same word usually written **sh,** the French word of the same spelling and meaning would be represented as *ma-sheen.* In this particular case the result is at most a tolerable version of the French, but much damage can be done where there is no direct equivalent in the two languages. If you do not know the correct pronunciation of the French word *pain*, you will certainly not know it any better by following an imitated version such as *pang*, since there is nothing in standard English equivalent to the nasal sound usually written as **in** in French.

The International Phonetic Alphabet is, as its name implies, a standard method of representing one sound by one symbol which is theoretically applicable to any language that may be described. Because it is standardized and followed in many language textbooks produced in many different languages it has the following advantages—

1. Although no system of representing spoken sounds by written symbols can be 100 per cent perfect, it is in its full form more detailed and therefore more accurate than any other system and is flexible enough to remain successful.

2. As part of its standard usage, anything written in I.P.A. is so indicated by being placed between square [brækits]: an additional reminder that nothing is to be read according to the orthographical rules of any particular language.

3. Because it is standardized there is no need to give a new key any time it is used.

4. If you have used the I.P.A. for learning one language, you will be able to turn to another language and get a fair idea of the similarities and differences between the two immediately.

This is not the place for a description of the I.P.A. in detail. If it is used in the textbook you are following, those parts of it which are relevant to the language will be explained in the introductory chapter. Since the basic principle of the system is "one sound, one symbol; one symbol, one sound," any further description would simply amount to describing symbols and sounds for particular languages. We should perhaps put the I.P.A. into perspective and sum up: an authentic accent can only be acquired by active imitation; it is possible to describe sounds and their formation on paper, but accent consists of more than the pronunciation of individual sounds; if any guide is given throughout the textbook in some sort of phonetic alphabet, the I.P.A. is the most reliable; but—if you are learning a new language, you are learning a new orthography, and learning a phonetic alphabet at the same time imposes an additional strain which, in the long run, may not be worth it. It is better to get a rough approximation of the sounds first, then a basic grasp of the language, and then to concentrate on the business of achieving a correct accent.

# CHAPTER 12

# USE OF GRAMMAR AND DICTIONARY

THE purpose of this chapter is primarily to suggest ways of overcoming the inevitable difficulties that ensue when there is no textbook specifically designed for self-tuition in the language you are learning. Its content may also prove useful in the event that the textbook you do have does not prove to be sufficiently comprehensive, clearly explained or well arranged to enable you to feel that you are making satisfactory progress or following a coherent and practical course. And even if you have a good textbook, some of these notes may be found handy for reference and revision planning. In other words, since you have got this far, you might as well read it anyway.

## How to Do Without a Textbook

A textbook, whatever method it follows, is designed to introduce vocabulary and grammatical constructions in easy and practical stages. If there is no such book available, it is still possible to gather this material from other sources—vocabulary from a dictionary, constructions from a grammar. You *must* have access to *both* of these, otherwise self-tuition is impossible. Since the elements and constructions given in a grammar, and the vocabulary given in a dictionary, follow a set and formalized pattern for ease of reference rather than a series of stages for practical learning, your main job is to select and order the given material, by stages, into something approaching textbook form. This involves extra work, of course, but with diligence it will enable you to overcome the problems of learning without a textbook.

Some sort of reader soon becomes an essential adjunct to the grammar and dictionary, for the reasons given in Chapter 6: it is of particular importance if you have no textbook since you will require many examples of connected text in the new language, which you are unlikely to find in a grammar. Newspapers or magazines would make satisfactory substitutes.

## Essential Vocabulary

Neither this nor the following section suggests a plan of *procedure*, (which is suggested in Chapter 1): each gives an outline of the *material,* which in practice may, but need not, follow the order in which it is presented here. Here follows, then, a survey of the essential elements of vocabulary which would form a sound basis for the practical knowledge of a foreign language.

PERSONAL NOUNS. The equivalents of *man, woman, boy, girl, person, people, child;* names of nationality and countries of those in which you are interested (i.e. relevant to the language being learnt); words appertaining to trades and professions, e.g., *grocer, baker, butcher, chemist, doctor, policeman, official, warden,* etc.; relatives, e.g., *wife, husband, mother, father, son, daughter, brother, sister,* and anyone else you may lose on holiday abroad.

IMPERSONAL NOUNS. Essential objects you may have on your person, in your room or place of work and use every day, ranging from *pen* and *pencil* to *typewriter* and *screwdriver;* words associated with travel, e.g. *car, train, bus, road, pavement, station, ticket, reservation, berth;* equivalents of *country, capital, city, town, village, sea, river;* essential buildings such as *hotel, garage, bank, post office,* and other similar categories.

ADJECTIVES. Of colour and texture, e.g. *red, yellow, blue, green, orange, brown, black, white, grey, plain, striped, spotted, light, dark;* of size, e.g. *big, small, long, short, tall, thin, thick, fat;* of form, e.g. *round, square, oblong, triangular;* of condition, e.g. *new, old, full, empty, clean, dirty, neat, worn, unused.* To these may be added less evident qualities of a subjective nature, e.g. *nice, horrible, pretty, ugly, ordinary, magnificent, peculiar, charming, stupid, disgusting.* The possessive adjectives, *my, your, his, her, our, their* are also an early essential group.

PRONOUNS. All the personal pronouns are necessary at an early stage. Particular attention must be paid in many languages to the equivalents of *you,* since few are as economical as English in this respect. Also important are *who, which, someone, no one, something, this one, that one, these, those.*

ADVERBS. Place: *where? (over) there, here, everywhere, nowhere, inside, outside, in front, behind, on top, underneath.*
    Time: *when? now, soon, recently, yesterday, today, tomorrow, always, often, occasionally, never, for a long time, early, late.*
    Quantity: *how much? a lot, a little, many, some, a few, too, very, almost, more, less, enough.*
    Manner: *how? quickly, slowly, easily, with difficulty, thus (= like this, like that).*

VERBS. Textbooks with a predominantly academic approach tend to introduce first sets of verbs which follow similar patterns of conjugation, that is the easy regular verbs, regardless of their degree of usage, and when dealing with irregular verbs are likely also to include many rare or archaic items which happen to follow a pattern being demonstrated. For a more practical approach it is essential to learn in addition to the "easy" verbs (the regular ones, which of course differ from language to language) a few verbs which may be "irregular" but which are fundamental to the basis of the language. Often it will be found that irregular verbs comprise those which are the commonest and those which are the rarest in use, while the majority of those in between are regular. Incidentally it is useful to note that in most languages any new verbs which are introduced simply as borrowings from another tongue or as technical vocabulary (e.g. *to televise*) based on word roots in current international usage, tend to be regular. There will not necessarily be one foreign verb for every English form given below—e.g. Spanish has two verbs equivalent to our *have* and another two equivalent to *to be*; Welsh has no verb *to have*—but the main point is to learn how phrases and sentences are formed in another language to signify ideas equivalent to those expressed by particular English verbs as follows—

*to be, have, seem, do, make, come, go, live, want, know, can, may, must;*

*to travel, arrive, return, enter, leave, go up* (= *mount*), *go down* (= *descend*);

*to look, see, listen, hear, speak, say, ask, reply, read, write, learn, remember, forget;*

*to lose, look for* (= *seek*), *find, take, get, give, buy, sell, put, keep, eat, work, sleep, sit down, stand up, wait for, open, close.*

PREPOSITIONS. It is in the realm of prepositions that languages show great differences of idiom, and they are often the most difficult parts of speech to translate accurately. For one thing, analytic languages make greater use of them than do the synthetic (*see* pages 24 and 97), and for another prepositional usage tends to vary not only from language to language but also from region to region: e.g. where English puts a picture "on" the wall, French puts it "at" the wall, and where one Englishman says "What do you think of it?" another says "What do you think *to* it?" The same caution therefore applies to prepositions as to verbs above: there may be more than one foreign preposition fulfilling the various functions of one in English and vice versa, and there may be a preposition in one language that has no equivalent at all in the other, which necessitates learning a particular phrase or construction, e.g. the German Dative *den Leuten*, which has no preposition, would in most cases be translated by the prepositional phrase *to the people* in English.

Basic prepositions and prepositional phrases in English: *to, at, near, by, from, of, with, without, before, after, for, because of, across, through, in, on, over, under, behind, in front of, between, to the right of, to the left of, along.*

CONJUNCTIONS. Some conjunctions in some languages (but not English) affect the form of the verb by requiring it to be in a certain "mood" (*see* page 92), so it is essential not to use a conjunction straight from the dictionary without checking its use in the grammar. The simplest and safest basic conjunctions are *and, or, but, because, for, as, when.*

NUMERALS. The cardinals (*one, two, three,* etc.) up to *twenty* to start with, and the ordinals *first, second, third* form an adequate basis.

OTHER WORDS. The articles *the, a, an,* if they are used, and their variations for number, gender and case.

The demonstrative adjectives *this, that, these, those,* and their variations as for articles.

The interrogatives *who? what? which?* and their variations as above, *where? when? how much* or *many? how? why?*

EVERYDAY PHRASES. Language at its barest is informative communication, at its noblest is an art, at its richest a medium of social intercourse. Few would hope to learn another language to produce great literature in it; many could learn enough to communicate essential information, but their speech would seem stark and impersonal. What turns the latter into sociable conversation are the knowledge and fluent use of well-worn phrases indicative of attention, politeness and personal feeling; expressions which are not an integral part of, but which, like spices, flavour the meat of any communication. Such phrases may belong to the realm of—

Information: *yes, no;*

Etiquette: (*yes*) *please,* (*no*) *thank you** *by all means, not at all, you're welcome, I beg your parden, sorry, excuse me, would you be so kind as to . . .?, could you please . . .?*

Greetings: *Hullo, good day* (and its component parts, if distinguished), *goodbye, how do you do, welcome to . . . , nice to see you;* and conventional letter forms;

Attention: *Of course, I see, quite* (*so*), *naturally, typical!, needless to say;*

* Usage varies from language to language. In *would you like another drink?—Thank you,* the *thank you* signifies *yes please,* whereas the equivalent *merci* in French signifies *no thank you.*

Modification: *As it were, so to speak;*
Ejaculation: *Really! Never! Good heavens! Well I'm . . .!*
Also in the category of phrases and expressions come those constructions indicating time and date, age, price, and basic weights and measures.

## GRAMMATICAL CONSTRUCTIONS AND SENTENCE PATTERNS

As we have noted, a grammar is likely to devote one chapter to each part of speech, an arrangement which does not facilitate learning since the minimum unit of learning material should be a complete sentence, which generally consists of at least noun and verb. Therefore you will need, if working from a grammar, to abstract a certain amount of information from each section from which you will be able to construct basic sentence patterns. Here follows, then, a survey of the material required and a suggestion for a series of types of sentence which should be included. The order in which they are given is not intended to reflect grades of ease and difficulty in sentence construction, since these vary from language to language; they range rather from basic essentials and simple sentences to elaborations and complex sentences. Although they need not be followed in the order given here, it should be obvious that many of the earlier constructions are more important than and fundamental to those mentioned later. It is obvious, for example, that the verb *to be*, or equivalent, is one of the most used in any language, and that the pattern consisting of subject/copula (some form of *be*)/complement is high on the list of practical essentials.

1. Type: Subject + Predicate based on verb **be**—

(*a*) Example: *The man is here.* Material: simple nouns restricted to the singular form, but varied to incorporate different genders or other classes. If the change from definite to indefinite article affects the form of the noun, construct a different pattern for each set, otherwise include both articles (if distinguished) in the same pattern. In respect of the verb it should be remembered that some languages (e.g. Spanish) have more than one equivalent of *to be*, and that when this occurs reference should be made to the grammar to find which is appropriate; also that some languages do not have or do not express the equivalent of *be* (e.g. Russian). The essential however is that this *type* of sentence, whatever its actual expression in that language, is bound to have *some* equivalent, and it is this equivalent which should be practised. For more adverbs of place, refer to page 80.

(*b*) Example: *The man is a doctor.* Material: as before, except that in this case the predicate includes more nouns, of for example, occupation, nationality.

(*c*) Example: *The man is rich.* Material: introduce now simple adjectives, incorporating in the pattern any change in the form of the adjective that may be made in respect of gender (i.e. agreement of adjectives).

(*d*) Example: *The man is a rich doctor.* Material: as before, save that the adjective is now immediately linked to a noun, in which case account has to be taken of word order (which comes first, noun or adjective?) and agreement if necessary.

(*e*) Example: *The rich doctor is here.* Material: as before, the adjective is now associated with the subject noun.

(*f*) Example: *The rich doctors are here.* Material: introduction of plural, which may affect the forms of the noun, the verb and the adjective.

(*g*) Using the same material, introduce the negative of the verb, thus ranging from *The man is not here* to *The rich doctors are not here.*

(*h*) Using the same material as before, introduce the interrogative, ranging from *Is the man here?* to *Are the rich doctors here?*

Items (*a*) to (*g*) should be practised as sentence patterns following the method described in Chapter 7. With the introduction of the interrogative forms and the equivalents of *yes* and *no*, the Question and Answer method can be used as a variation.

It will be seen that the first stage introduces the fundamentals of any language: question, affirmative statement, negative statement, articles, gender, number, use of adjectives (agreement and order). Where case is distinguished, only the Nominative has been used. The closer the foreign language is to English in construction, the easier and quicker this stage will be. Where the foreign language shows peculiarities (e.g. enclitic article in Scandinavian languages, mutation in Celtic, plural forms in German, etc.), special attention must be paid to these points as they arise.

2. Type: Subject + "to have" equivalent + direct object—

(*a*) Example: *The doctor has a house.* Material: equivalent of the English verb *to have* in the sense of *possess*. The equivalent may not be a similar verb (as in Welsh, which says for the above *There is a house with the doctor*), or there may be need to choose between two dictionary equivalents (e.g. Spanish distinguishes *tener* = *to have, possess, hold* from *haber* which is used in the construction of the perfect tense, as in *the doctor has finished*). Introduction is also made of the Accusative case in those languages which formally distinguish cases.

(*b*) Example: *I have a house*. Material: introduce personal pronouns as subjects, and practise these also with the verb *to be*.

(*c*) As before, practise negative and interrogative forms.

3. Type: Subject + "To give" equivalent + Direct Object + Indirect Object—

(*a*) Example: *I give the woman a present/I give a present to the woman*. Material: Introduction is here made of either the Dative case (if this is formally distinguished), or a preposition equivalent to *to*, and attention should be paid to word order (whether direct precedes indirect or vice-versa). As before, negative and interrogative should be introduced.

(*b*) Example: *I give her it/I give it to her*. Material: introduce direct and indirect object pronouns. This is a tricky point in any language—do not attempt them all at once.

In these two stages, the introduction of pronouns and of the distinction between direct and indirect objects (made in most European languages and expressed in some by the Accusative and Dative cases) very nearly completes the basic stock of grammatical processes and constructions which form the framework of the whole language. Excluding verbs for the moment, additional items include (i) formation of the possessive (use of the Genitive in those languages distinguishing formal "cases"), (ii) the construction of adverbial phrases of place, time and manner—this involves the use of prepositions in most languages and the remaining "cases" (e.g. instrumental, locative, etc.) in some, (iii) other types of pronouns—possessive, demonstrative, interrogative, etc.

In the acquisition of verbs two processes should be followed at the same time, appertaining respectively to the questions "what verbs to learn" and "what forms to learn." In the former, the stages should be as follows: (1) to be, have, give; (2) other commonly used and therefore practically essential verbs (refer to the list on page 81); (3) verbs following regular patterns or "conjugations"; (4) any others which you then come across in reading passages and work based on use of books and periodicals. In the latter, the direction should be (1) tense or tenses equivalent to the English Present; (2) Past tense(s); (3) Future and Conditional or equivalents; (4) the Passive voice or equivalent methods of expressing the passive in English; (5) any other tenses, or moods such as Subjunctive, Imperative, Optative, etc.

# CHAPTER 13

# A HUNDRED GRAMMATICAL TERMS
## EXPLAINED

THE purpose of the following glossary is twofold. Firstly, it is to offer an explanation and example of any individual grammatical term that may be used in textbooks on any of the major languages of Europe. For the most part, the terms relate to concepts which are expressed in several different languages, since these are the ones most likely to be taken for granted by textbook authors. Noun cases such as *illative, elative, adessive*, etc., which are peculiar to one language, will of course most probably be dealt with quite thoroughly in the textbook, and need not find their place here. Secondly, it is hoped that the cross-references and, in some cases, repeated explanations under different headings, may help in the understanding of concepts in relation to one another rather than merely in isolation. For example, *subjunctive* is explained under *mood*, so that its characteristics may be compared with those of other moods, and again under *verb*, in which the relation of *mood* to other verbal ideas (*tense, aspect*, etc.) can also be seen.

An item in small capital letters in the course of an entry indicates that the word itself also forms a separate entry. For *intransitive, irregular* and so on, see *transitive, regular*, etc.

### GLOSSARY OF GRAMMATICAL TERMS

**Abstract noun:** one which denotes a state, feeling or quality rather than a physical thing, e.g. *life, hope, precision*, etc. In many languages these are derived from adjectives, verbs or other nouns by means of distinctive endings, e.g. Eng. *one—oneness*, Ger. *ein(s) —Einheit*, Fre. *un—unité*.

**Accusative case:** the state of a noun or pronoun which forms the DIRECT OBJECT of a verb.

**Active:** *see* VOICE.

**Adjective:** a word which describes, qualifies or modifies a noun in a particular instance, e.g. *green* in *a green house, house* in *a house coat*. A phrase may be adjectival, e.g. *the never-ending night*.

**Adverb:** a word or phrase which serves to describe, qualify or modify any part of speech other than a noun, usually a verb or adjective, e.g. *he spoke quite openly, he was openly helpful*. An adverb answers the questions *how, when, where?*

**Affirmative:** the form of a phrase or sentence which *makes a statement*, as distinct from an INTERROGATIVE which *asks a question*.

**Affix:** modifying syllable(s) directly attached to a word, e.g. *-less* and *-ness* in the compound *sleeplessness*. These are suffixes; prefixes are affixed to the beginning of the word, e.g. *fix, affix, prefix, suffix*.

**Analytic:** a method of denoting grammatical relations by analysing them into their constituent parts and expressing each part in the form of a separate word or distinctive element. Opposite of SYNTHETIC, *see* Chapter 3.

**Animate:** and **inanimate:** self-explanatory. In some languages words denoting animate things may be used or formed differently from those inanimate, and the distinction between the two, linguistically, may not always correspond to the logical or factual distinction.

**Article:** in English, *the* (definite article), *a(n)* (indefinite article), and matched by several European languages. French distinguishes a plural indefinite article (*des maisons* = *houses*, plural of *a house*); some distinguish definite but not indefinite (Welsh *y tŷ* = *the house*, *tŷ* = *a house*); some neither (Russian *dom* = *house, a house, the house*).

**Aspect:** the aspect of a verb, generally, denotes the nature of performance of the action, e.g. *I am going* is continuous in aspect; *I keep on going* is iterative in aspect; *I used to go* is habitual.

**Attributive:** the adjective *fierce* is attributive in *the natives are fierce*, and epithetic in *the fierce natives are here* or *these are fierce natives*. The distinction can be of importance, e.g. in German an adjective used epithetically must agree with the noun described, but an attributive one is invariable.

**Auxiliary verb:** one which helps another verb in the formation of tenses, voices, aspects, etc.; e.g. *be, have, do, keep* in *I am writing, I have written, I do write, I keep writing*.

**Cardinal numbers:** the numerals used in counting (*one, two, three*, etc.), as distinct from the ordinals (*first, second, third*).

**Case:** the state of a noun according to its use in a phrase or sentence, e.g. if it is the subject of a verb it is said to be in the *nominative case*. Such terminology is usually only employed in respect of languages which distinguish the case of a noun by a particular ending. For details, see ACCUSATIVE, DATIVE, GENITIVE, INSTRUMENTAL, NOMINATIVE, PREPOSITIONAL.

**Clause:** a phrase containing a finite verb, equivalent to a simple sentence though perhaps forming part of a complex sentence, e.g. *He came in,/sat down,/and began to dictate a letter* consists of three clauses. *He came in* is a main clause. *He began to dictate a letter* is a main clause, but, connected by the link-word *and* in the above example, is described as a co-ordinate clause together with the others. A subordinate clause, which may be marked in some languages by a modification to the verb or by a distinct word order, is one which is attached to a main clause by a subordinative conjunction (e.g. perhaps equivalent to *although, because,* etc.) and is thought to be dependent for its full sense upon the main clause. This is more a purely grammatical than a logical distinction, and different languages vary in their interpretation of a Subordinate Clause. RELATIVE CLAUSES (q.v.) are subordinate.

**Collective noun:** one which is singular in form but plural in meaning, e.g. *the herd, the élite,* etc.

**Common:** a gender, or class of nouns, equivalent to *masculine* and/or *feminine* as opposed to *neuter.* The terms correspond roughly with *animate* and *inanimate,* but the distinction between the two is more often a grammatical convention than a logical necessity. (*See* **gender.**)

**Comparative:** the state of an adjective in the making of a comparison, e.g. *big,* comparative form *bigger; enjoyable,* comparative form *more enjoyable. See* also SUPERLATIVE and EQUATIVE. Where the distinction is relevant, the basic form (*big, enjoyable*) is referred to as *positive.*

**Concord** or **agreement:** an arrangement whereby the form of a word is modified to show direct application or relation to a noun or pronoun. In English only verbs are made to "agree" with their subject nouns, e.g. in *the cow ruminates,* the verb bears an **-s** which marks the singularity of *cow;* in *the cows ruminate,* the plurality of *cow* is marked by a zero modification (lack of ending) in the verb. In many languages, adjectives are modified according to the number and gender of the noun they describe (*see* page 25).

**Conditional:** the state or MOOD of a verb when the action expressed by the verb is regarded as a hypothesis rather than as a definite fact. For example, in *I would buy it if I had the money, would buy* is the conditional form of *buy,* the action being regarded as dependent on the condition suggested by the clause introduced by *if.*

**Conjugation:** the systematic statement of all the forms that a verb may take according to all possible circumstances constitutes its conjugation. If several verbs follow the same pattern of formal modifications, then they are said to be *regular* in respect of that pattern or conjugation.

**Conjunction:** a word (or phrase) which links one clause to another. For example the clauses *He is rich. He is ugly,* may be linked together by conjunctions such as *and, but, although, because, in spite of the fact that,* etc. A co-ordinative conjunction (e.g. *and*) produces two clauses which are of equal and independent significance; a subordinative conjunction (e.g. *because*) introduces a clause which is subordinate to or dependent for its significance on the other. Thus—

    *He is rich and he is ugly.* } Co-ordinative: no difference in
    *He is ugly and he is rich.* }   meaning.
    *He is rich because he is ugly.* } Sub-ordinative: difference in
    *He is ugly because he is rich.* }   meaning.

**Continuous:** the ASPECT (q.v.) of a verb by which is expressed the fact that the action described is regarded as continuous or unfinished (i.e. incomplete or *imperfect*—the latter being the more usual grammatical term). Contrast: *He was winning* (continuous or imperfect)/*He won* (completed or perfect).

**Co-ordinative:** *see* CONJUNCTION, CLAUSE.

**Dative:** the state or CASE of a noun or pronoun which forms the INDIRECT OBJECT or a verb.

**Declension:** the systematic description of all the forms that a noun or pronoun may take according to the differing grammatical functions it may have in the sentence, e.g. the forms indicating NUMBER (singular and plural), or CASE, q.v. In languages whose nouns vary little or not at all in form (analytic languages, *see* page 24), the term *declension* is of no significance. In (generally more synthetic) languages in which the adjective changes form to match that of the noun it describes, the adjective also has a declension.

**Defective:** a verb whose conjugation is lacking in some forms. For example English *must* has no past tense, instead we resort to the phrases *had to, was obliged to,* etc. *Must* is therefore defective.

**Definite:** a noun is the name given to a member of a class of persons, objects or ideas, e.g. *book* denotes any one of a whole class of similar but not identical objects. If the object spoken about has already been introduced, or is defined as a particular member, its noun is *definite,* and in many languages is preceded by the *definite article,* e.g. *the book* (one which is to be defined immediately, or has already been defined). If, however, *any* member of the class is to be referred to, its noun is indefinite and may be preceded by an *indefinite article* (e.g. *a book*).

**Demonstrative:** a word which singles out and draws attention to a particular object (which thus becomes DEFINITE, *see* above). It may be an adjective, e.g. *this book, that book,* or a PRONOUN (q.v.) e.g. *this is the one, that is the one.*

**Direct object:** a noun or pronoun which is directly affected by the action of a verb, e.g. *book* in *he bought the book*, or *he wrote the book*.

**Direct speech:** *see* SPEECH.

**Dual:** we denote the plural of most nouns in English by adding -*s*, e.g. *eye*, *eyes*. In some languages the noun has a special form indicating two of an object, as if we said, for example, *one eye*, *many eyes* but *two eyen*. *Eyen* would in such a case be the dual of *eye*.

**Epithetic:** an adjective used epithetically is one which is attached directly to its noun to form a noun phrase. Opposite of ATTRIBU-TIVE, q.v.

**Equative:** *as good as* is the equative form of the adjective *good*. *See also* COMPARATIVE, SUPERLATIVE.

**Feminine:** *see* GENDER.

**Future:** the state or tense of a verb whose action takes place in the future, e.g. *he will go* is the future tense of *he goes*. This distinction is not as obvious as it appears. In English, for example, we may use a future tense to express the present in, e.g. *he will be there by now*, and the present tense to express the future in, e.g. (*I will see him*) *when he comes* (the French would say *when he will come*).

**Gender:** theoretically, anything which is male is of the masculine gender; which is female, of the feminine gender; and which is neither, of the neuter gender. In practice, however, the term *gender* has a grammatical usage which is rarely consistent with objective reality. A language which distinguishes all three genders (e.g. German) does so sometimes on the basis of reality (*der Mann*, masculine; *die Frau = the woman*, feminine; *das Ding = the thing*, neuter), sometimes obviously on the basis of the actual form of the word (e.g. any noun taking the diminutive endings -*lein*, -*chen* is neuter, thus *das Fräulein*, from *die Frau*; *das Mädchen = girl* from *die Magd*), sometimes for no obvious reason (*der Stein = stone*, masc.; *die Feder = feather*, fem.; *das Pferd = horse*, neut.). Similarly for a language distinguishing only two genders: French has no neuter so all items are either masculine or feminine, whether by meaning (*un homme*, *une femme*), or by form (words ending in -*elle* are fem., so *la sentinelle = sentry*, fem.); Swedish distinguishes *neuter* but opposes this with a *common* gender, representing a coalescence of masculine with feminine—but still, *en fjäder = feather*, common; *ett djur = animal*, neut. English does not distinguish grammatical gender. By this we mean that real or "logical" gender does not affect the form of words or the sentences in which they occur, for e.g. *conductress* is simply a different word from *conductor* and, apart from the change of *he* to *she*, any sentence containing one remains unaltered when the other is substituted. In languages which do distinguish gender, however, the substitution of a masculine for a feminine word is likely to necessitate formal changes in any articles, adjectives or even verbs associated with the noun (*see* page 56).

**Genitive:** basically, the state or case of a noun when it is held to be the possessor of an associated noun; also called possessive, and *see* page 22. In languages which distinguish the genitive case by a particular form, however, the genitive may have other uses, e.g. in German after the preposition *wegen: wegen des Regens =  because of the rain* (genitive of *Regen*).

**Idiom:** a phrase, or group of words, peculiar to a particular language and which cannot (except by coincidence) therefore be translated literally (e.g. *all over the place = anywhere* or *everywhere* or *untidy; to put up = to lodge; to put up with = to bear*): Compare PHRASE.

**Imperative:** the state or MOOD of a verb when it is used to give an order or direct prohibition, e.g. *go home* or *do not spit*.

**Imperfect:** *see* CONTINUOUS.

**Indefinite:** *see* DEFINITE, and PRONOUN.

**Indicative:** the MOOD of a verb when the action described is regarded as real or definite.

**Indirect object:** theoretically, the state of a noun which is considered to be the recipient or benefiting party in respect of a verbal activity, e.g. *me* in *he gave me a chance, he read me a letter, he got me a job*. The indirect object may be distinguished by a preposition (English *to me, for me*) or by the dative case (German *mir*, distinct from the accusative or direct object form *mich*).

**Indirect speech:** *see* SPEECH.

**Infinitive:** the MOOD of a verb when the action is not pinned down to a definite person, time or nature; the name of the verb; e.g. *to go, to return*.

**Inflexion:** a modification in the basic form of a word to express a grammatical relation, e.g. from *king*, *kings* is an inflected form showing the plural, *king's* an inflected form showing the genitive or possessive case; from *live, lived* is inflected to show past time. (*See also* page 22.)

**Instrumental:** the state or case of a noun or pronoun when it denotes the means by which an action is performed. It may be distinguished by a preposition (English: *to cut with a knife*) or by a distinctive instrumental case.

**Interjection:** a word immediately expressive of some direct emotion, e.g. *ouch!*

**Interrogative:** either a questioning word (*e.g. who? when? which?*), or the form of a verb when making a question rather than a statement (e.g. *do you see?* interrogative form of *you see*). (*See also* PRONOUN.)

**Masculine:** *see* GENDER.

**Mood:** the state of a verb in accordance with the degree of reality or definiteness associated by the speaker with it.

    *Infinitive:* the general idea of the verb, unrestricted by person or time, generally marked in English by a preceding *to*, e.g. *to do, to see, to run.* All other moods are *finite*.

    *Imperative:* the form of a verb used in giving an order or making a prohibition, e.g. *look at that!*

    *Subjunctive:* the form of a verb when the action is regarded as unreal, hypothetical, or dependent on a wish or desire. Not clearly marked in English, but may be seen in *I wish I were there.* In some languages the subjunctive is used to give a sort of indirect order, as in *may they die of shame, let him now approach* (jussive subjunctive).

    *Conditional:* more "real" than in the subjunctive, the action is regarded as dependent on a given condition: *if he were here* (subjunctive, purely hypothetical) *he would confirm it* (conditional, dependent on previous condition).

    *Indicative:* in which direct statements or questions are made (e.g. *is he here? he will confirm it*). This is the most commonly used mood.

**Negative:** either a word which negates (*no money, not out!, never again*) or the form of a verb in which a statement is negated, though this is usually done by means of a distinct negative word (*he will not come; to be or not to be*).

**Neuter:** *see* GENDER.

**Nominative:** the state or CASE of a noun or pronoun when it is the SUBJECT of a verb.

**Noun:** anything about which a statement can be made, i.e. which can be the subject of a sentence, for example, the first word in each of the following sentences: *man does not live by bread alone, green is a cool colour, walking is good for the digestion.* In English, the fact that *green* is normally an adjective, and *walking* a verb, does not prevent them from being used as nouns provided some sense is made; however, not all languages are so flexible and it is not safe to use what are normally adjectives, verbs, etc., as nouns *ad lib.* A noun may change its form or be modified by the addition of another word to express NUMBER, GENDER, or CASE, qq.v.

**Number:** the distinction between singular and plural, e.g. (*one*) *eye,* (*many*) *eyes;* (*one*) *man,* (*many*) *men.* Some languages also distinguish a DUAL number (q.v.). In some languages a plural noun remains in the singular form when preceded by a numeral (Welsh: *dyn, dynion* = *man, men,* but *tri dyn, three men*). Most languages have some collective nouns, by which plurality may be expressed by a word in the singular form (*see* COLLECTIVE). A change in the number of a noun may affect the form of any associated adjectives or verbs in the sentence (*see* CONCORD); to this extent adjectives and verbs may also be said to express number.

**Numerals:** The *cardinal* numerals (*one, two, three,* etc.) may be used as adjectives (e.g. *three men*), in which case some languages may require the numeral to "agree" with its noun; as nouns (e.g. *three and five are eight*), these being the usual forms for simply counting; or as pronouns (e.g. *one chopped himself in half and then there were six*). The *ordinal* numerals denote position in sequence (*first, second, third,* etc.) and may be used as adjectives or pronouns.

**Object:** the goal of the action of a verb; *see* DIRECT and INDIRECT object.

**Optative:** the subjunctive MOOD of a verb, q.v., when the action of the verb is considered to be hypothetical and dependent on a verb of *wishing,* etc.

**Ordinal:** *first, second, third,* etc., are the ordinal numeral adjectives, *firstly,* etc., the ordinal adverbs. (*See* NUMERALS.)

**Paradigm:** a systematic statement or representation in tabular form of all the formal variations applicable to a basic word or type of word for a given grammatical situation: the following is the paradigm for the German verb *kommen* (*to come*) in the *present tense*—

| | |
|---|---|
| ich komme | wir kommen |
| du kommst | ihr kommt |
| er kommt | sie kommen |

**Participle:** part of a verb from which may be formed other tenses, voices, aspects, etc., of the verb itself, or other parts of speech. English distinguishes a present and a past participle. The present participle ends in *-ing* and forms (1) the continuous aspect, e.g. *I am thinking, I was thinking, I shall be thinking, I may have been thinking,* etc.; (2) a verbal noun, e.g. *thinking doesn't agree with me, I am allergic to thinking;* (3) an adjective, e.g. *man is a thinking animal;* (4) an adverb, e.g. *he entered, thinking he was late.* The past (or passive) participle forms (1) the perfect aspect or tenses, e.g. *I have thought of something, who would have thought it?* (2) the passive voice, e.g. *he is thought to be dead, this was thought stupid;* (3) an adjective, e.g. *a well conceived strategy*. Most European languages possess a combined past/passive participle, used in similar ways to the English; present participles are more restricted. Future participles are rarely found in modern languages (Latin: *morituri te salutamus: (we)-who-are-about-to-die salute you*, from *morior = to die*). The use of participles is usually a tricky point in any language.

**Particle:** specifically, particles are invariable parts of speech such as prepositions, conjunctions and interjections. Generally, a particle is the term given to a word that has little or no intrinsic meaning but has a grammatical function. (*See* page 22.)

**Partitive:** French grammarians refer to their *du, de la, des* as partitive articles ( = English *some*, in *some money, some people*). In *some of the time, some* is a partitive pronoun, *of the time* is the phrase denoting the partitive genitive of *time*. This is one special use of the GENITIVE (q.v.) in languages which distinguish that case formally. (*See also* PRONOUN.)

**Passive:** *see* VERB.

**Past:** *see* TENSE and PARTICIPLE.

**Perfect:** = finished, completed; *see* PARTICIPLE.

**Person:** the speaker or writer is the *first person* (pronoun *I*, plural *we*); the person or personified object addressed directly by the speaker is the *second person* (pronoun *you*); everything spoken about is *third person* (pronouns *he, she, it*, plural *they*). (*See also* PRONOUN.)

**Phrase:** a group of words conveying a single idea. *Philip* is a noun; *Duke of Edinburgh* is a noun- (or substantival) phrase. *Sunny* is an adjective; *sun-drenched* is an adjectival phrase. *Here* is an adverb; *on this very spot* an adverbial phrase. *To finish* is a verb; *to get it over with* a verbal phrase. Some phrases which mean more than the sum of their parts, or are used metaphorically, become IDIOMS, q.v. Note e.g.—

    1. He is mad. (One-word adjective with equivalent in other languages.)

    2. He is mentally defective. (Adjectival phrase, each word used literally so can probably be translated word for word.)

    3. He is round the bend. (Adjectival phrase peculiar to English, each word used metaphorically, therefore an *idiom* and cannot be literally translated.)

**Plural:** = more than one. (*See* NUMBER.)

**Possessive:** (*see* GENITIVE CASE and page 22). The *possessive adjectives* are *my, your, his, her, its*, etc.; the *possessive pronouns* are *mine, yours, his, hers*, etc.

**Predicate:** that part of the sentence which contains the verb and everything immediately associated with it; says something about the SUBJECT *see* SENTENCE.

**Prefix:** an element affixed or attached to the beginning of a word to modify its meaning or grammatical function, e.g. **re-** in *redevelop*, etc. (*See also* AFFIX.)

**Preposition:** a word (particle) or phrase denoting the relationship, either physical or grammatical or both, of one word to another, e.g.—

> *with: he arrived* with *a friend* (denotes physical relationship of accompaniment),
>
> *whom he killed* with *a hammer* (denotes INSTRUMENTAL case, q.v.)
>
> with *great gusto* (*great* adjective, *gusto* noun, *great gusto* noun phrase, *with great gusto* forms an adverbial phrase —an adverb being that which answers the question *how? in what way? with* is therefore a particle serving a purely grammatical function).

**Prepositional case:** the form of a noun which is governed by a preposition (as e.g. *friend, hammer, gusto* in above examples) in those languages where such a distinction is actually made.

**Present:** *see* TENSE and PARTICIPLE.

**Pronoun:** a word which stands for, replaces or represents a noun. Personal: *I, you, he,* etc. Possessive: *mine, yours, his,* etc. Reflexive: *myself, yourself, himself,* etc. Interrogative: *who? what? which one?* Demonstrative: *this* (*one*), *that* (*one*), *these,* etc. Relative: *who, which, that* (introducing a relative clause). Indefinite: *someone, something, anyone,* etc. Partitive: *some* (*of*), *few* (*of*), *many* (*of*), etc. Numerals may also be used as pronouns (*see* that entry).

**Proper noun:** one which takes the form of a personal or place name. Most nouns denote one of a set of similar objects, e.g. *book* is the noun relating to a variety of objects falling in that category. A proper noun denotes a unique object or person—e.g. *the Good Book,* meaning *Bible,* is in that context a proper noun. In English proper nouns are written with a capital initial, as well as adjectives derived from them, e.g. *Shaw, Shavian, Belgium, Belgian.* Other languages vary in use. French, for example, has an initial capital only with the primary name, not with derivatives, hence *France, français,* even where the latter means *a Frenchman.* German has an initial capital with every noun, proper or otherwise.

**Reflexive:** *see* VERB and PRONOUN.

**Regular:** any part of speech which is capable of being modified or formally changed is regular if the changes it undergoes follow a pattern applicable to other words constituting the same part of speech. For example, the normal method of indicating plural of a noun in English is by adding **-s** (*house, houses; tree, trees*). A noun pluralized by any other method (*man, men; foot, feet*) is irregular.

**Relative:** a *relative pronoun* (*see* PRONOUN) is one which refers back to something already mentioned and forms part of a new (relative) clause. For example, in the last sentence, *which* refers back to the pronoun *one* (in itself standing for the word "pronoun") and forms the subject of the verb *refers*. The clause *which refers back to something already mentioned* is therefore a relative clause. Since that clause cannot stand by itself as a complete sentence, it is *subordinate*, as all relative clauses are. (*See* CLAUSE.)

**Root:** the root of a word is its minimum significant part, that is, that which carries the basic meaning. For example, of the words *sing, singing, sang, sung, song*, the root is *s-ng*. An etymological root is the earliest known or inferred form of a particular word, e.g. English *five*, German *fünf*, French *cinq*, Cornish *pymp*, Russian *pjat'*, Latin *quinque* are derived from a prehistoric form which was probably something like *penk(w)e*.

**Sentence:** in practice, a minimum complete utterance, e.g. *Help!/Go away!/Dogs bite/Typical carnivores of the genus Canis display a regrettable tendency to insert their dental accoutrements into one's flesh.* In grammatical theory, a sentence is produced when a subject, or thing-to-be-spoken-about, is selected (e.g. *dogs*, or *typical carnivores of the genus Canis*), and a predicate is attached, i.e. something is said about it (e.g. *bite*, and the rest of the other one). A simple sentence contains one verb in the indicative, and is also a clause. A compound sentence contains several clauses (e.g. *dogs bite because they like human flesh* contains two clauses, as indicated by the presence of two verbs).

**Singular:** *see* NUMBER.

**Speech, direct and indirect:** Direct speech is represented when the actual words are quoted, e.g. *He said "I'm ill."* Indirect speech reports the statement at second hand, e.g. *He said he was ill.* Languages may formally indicate indirect speech by e.g. a conjunction (*He said THAT he was ill*) or word order or by special treatment of the verb.

**Stem:** the basic form of a word, to which endings or modifications are added. Not necessarily the same as ROOT (q.v.): *singing* is formed by adding a modification to the stem *sing*, which is in itself a variant of the root *s-ng*.

**Strong:** in Germanic languages, roughly equivalent to irregular in respect of verbs. (*See* WEAK.)

**Subject:** what is spoken about, is the subject; what is said about it, is the predicate; *see* SENTENCE, e.g. *dogs bite* is a statement about dogs, *dogs* being the subject, *bite* the predicate. *How lofty are thy mansions* is a statement about *thy mansions,* which are therefore the subject, the predicate being *are how lofty.* Note how the subject changes in these sentences—

> *I gave him a playful push with a pikestaff* (subject, verb, indirect object, direct object, instrument);
> *A playful push was given to him by me, with a pikestaff* (subject, verb, indirect object, agent, instrument);
> *He was given a playful push with a pikestaff, by me* (subject, verb, direct object, instrument, agent).

**Subjunctive:** *see* MOOD.
**Subordinate:** *see* CONJUNCTION and CLAUSE.
**Substantive:** in practice, the equivalent of a NOUN, q.v.
**Suffix:** an element which may be added to the end of a word to modify or amplify its meaning or grammatical function, e.g. *-ing. See* AFFIX.
**Superlative:** *biggest* is the superlative form of *big, best* the superlative of *good, most enjoyable* the superlative of *enjoyable.* (*See also* COMPARATIVE.)
**Synthetic:** a method of denoting grammatical relations by modifying the form of the words in a sentence. (*See* page 24.)
**Tense:** means "time." Compare—

1. He says "It was raining." (Past tense.)
2. He says "It is raining." (Present tense.)
3. He says "It will be raining." (Future tense.)

A verb is in the present tense when by its form it indicates that the action described is contemporaneous with the making of the statement (2, above). An action which is regarded as taking place before the statement was made is in the past tense, and one regarded as due to take place later, in the future tense. Unfortunately the notion of tense is generally confused with the notion of ASPECT. Thus *it was raining, it rained, it used to rain* are all types of past tense—they could be called, respectively, Past Tense Continuous Aspect, Past Tense Definite Aspect, Past Tense Habitual Aspect. As it happens, however, the notion of aspect is not very clearly marked in most European languages (there are other languages in which aspect is more carefully distinguished than tense). Therefore it has become customary to refer to any separate distinction of aspect as a tense in itself. Thus in French we have *il plut* (*it rained*), a definite completed action in the past, and *il pleuvait* (it was raining), a continuous or incompleted action in the past. In French it is only when referring to past time that such a distinction of aspect is made, for the present *it rains* and *it is raining* are alike expressed by *il pleut*. Thus *il pleut* is called the Present Tense, *il pleuvait* the Imperfect Tense, *il plut* the Past Historic Tense, thereby obscuring the basic notion of tense as meaning time. Similarly, the Conditional is also confusingly known as a tense, when it is in fact a MOOD (q.v.). When you are introduced to a verbal tense in a textbook it is essential to note (1) whether the tense relates to past, present, or future, and (2) what aspect is also implied, that is exactly in what circumstances it is used, and how the equivalent is expressed in English.

**Transitive:** a verb which takes a DIRECT OBJECT is transitive.

**Verb:** the essential core of a predicate; the word or phrase which says something about the subject; generally expressive of an action, state, process or feeling: e.g. *to go, to strike, to look* (action); *to be, to seem* (state); *to grow, to become* (process); *to wish, to hope* (feeling). The actual form of a verb may vary or be modified to express different grammatical circumstances or relationships, namely—

> *Concord:* it may be required to agree with the subject, i.e. change form according to the person, gender or number of the noun or pronoun governing it; cf. *I do, he does.*
>
> *Tense:* it may show by its forms whether the action takes place in the past, or present, or future, in relation to the time when the statement is made.
>
> *Aspect:* it may show by its form whether the action is envisaged as a continuous process (= imperfect), a completed action (perfect), habitual, intermittent, etc.
>
> *Mood:* it may show by its form to what extent the speaker regards the action as real, or hypothetical, e.g. *I come, I would come if. . . , I may come.*
>
> *Voice:* the verb is active if the subject is the agent or performer of the action (e.g. *he strikes*), passive if the subject is the recipient (e.g. *he is struck*).
>
> *Participles:* the verb may have forms used in conjunction with auxiliary verbs to form other tenses, aspects, moods, voices (e.g. *strike*, past tense and passive participle *struck: he has struck, he is struck*), or to form other parts of speech.

*See also* individual entries. A verb is—

> *Auxiliary* if it aids another verb in the formation of tense, mood, etc. (e.g. *have, be, can* in *I have struck, I have been striking,*

*I have been struck, I can strike, I can have been struck,* etc.);

*Affirmative* if it states a positive fact or possibility;

*Defective* if it is lacking in certain tenses (e.g., *must*);

*Impersonal* if there is no logical subject (e.g., *it rains, it looks nice out*);

*Interrogative* if it requests rather than states information (e.g., *Is he here?*);

*Intransitive* if it cannot take a direct object (e.g., *to go, to listen*);

*Irregular* if the modifications it undergoes differ from those of other verbs (e.g., *look, looked; seem, seemed;* but *buy, bought*);

*Negative* when it negates, denies or expresses the opposite of its basic meaning, in English always by means of the particle *not;*

*Reflexive* when the direct object is in reality the same person as the subject (e.g., *I wash myself*);

*Regular* if it follows a standard pattern of endings or other modifications;

*Transitive* if it takes a DIRECT OBJECT (q.v.).

**Voice:** = active or passive, *see* VERB.

**Weak:** in Germanic languages (English, Dutch, German, and Scandinavian) a verb may form its past tense in one of two ways: (1) by the addition of a dental sound (**d, t, th**) e.g. English *live, lived,* German *leben, lebt-;* (2) by modification of the root vowel, e.g. English *sing, sang,* German *singen, sang.* Those of type (1) are called weak verbs, of type (2) are called strong verbs. Some weak verbs are irregular, e.g. *lead, led; dream, dreamt.* Strong verbs can be grouped according to the nature of the vowel change, and a strong verb might be regarded as regular if it fits into a particular category, irregular if it has peculiarities. Thus "weak" and "strong" are not entirely synonymous with "regular" and "irregular."

# INDEX

(For grammatical terms *see* Glossary, pages 86–99)

ABKAZ, 14
Accent (diacritic mark), 76
Accent (pronunciation), 74, 75, 76, 77, 78
Africa, 9, 10
Agglutinative languages, 24
Ainu, 11
Alphabet, 73, 76–8
Analytic languages, 24, 89
Andaman isles, 11
Arabic, 7, 8, 12, 15
Asia, 9
Aspects of verb, 41
Australia, 9, 11

BACKGROUND, 66–7
Bantu languages, 10
Basque, 7, 11, 12
Belgium, 9
Bengali, 8
Borneo, 10
Brazil, 9
Bulgarian, 18

CANADA, 9
Catalan, 7, 11, 12
Caucasian languages, 12, 14
Celtic languages, 41, 59, 84
Central America, 9
Child, ability of to learn language, 27–9
China, 8, 10
Chinese, 8, 15, 41
Cognate words, 19
Connotation, 20
Conversation, 4
Cornish, 96
Cyrillic, 76
Czech, 18

DANISH, 7, 16
Denotation, 20
Dictionaries, 21, 44–5, 79–85
Direct method, 34–5
Dutch, 12, 17, 33, 99

ENGLISH, 8–9, 12, 14, 15, 16, 17, 18, 33, 62, 63, 73, 75, 76, 77, 78, 87–96, *passim*, 98, 99
Eskimo, 14
Estonian, 8

Evening classes, 34
Exercises, 4, 43–4

*Faux amis*, 20
Figurative use of words, 21
Films, 40, 49
Flexions, 16, 22–4
Fluency, 31
France, 9, 11
French, 7, 8, 9, 11, 14, 15, 16, 17, 18, 53–6, 62, 63–4, 73, 75, 76, 77, 78, 82, 87, 90, 94, 95, 96, 97

GERMAN, 8, 11, 12, 17, 56–8, 59, 62, 63, 64, 76, 82, 84, 87, 90, 91, 93, 95, 96, 99
Gothic script, 76
Grammars, 40, 45–6, 79–85
Grammatical structure, 22, 83–5
Greek, 11, 17, 34, 76

HEBREW, 11
Hindi, 8
Homonyms, 20
Hungarian, 9

ICELANDIC, 73
Idioms, 25
Imitated pronunciation, 31, 42, 47
India, 8, 9
Indirect method, 34–5
Indo-China, 10
Indonesian, 11
Inflexions, 16
International Phonetic Alphabet, 41, 76–8
Interrogative words, basic, 62
Intonation, 74, 75
Irish, 7
Italian, 8, 11, 18

JAPANESE, 7, 8, 11, 15, 18
Java, 10

KURDISH, 7, 11

LANGUAGE laboratories, 36
Languages,
    distribution, 7
    number, 7
Lappish, 9

Latin, 17, 18, 34, 94, 96
Latin languages, 18
Lingua franca, 9–11
Linguistic prejudice, 29–30
Literal use of words, 21

MALAY, 8, 9, 10, 12, 43
Meaning, 19–21
Method of work, 5–6
Mother tongue, 27–9
Motivation, 30
Mutation, 41

NATIVE speakers, 49
North America, 9
Norwegian, 41

ORAL practice, 39
Organs of speech, 77

PACIFIC, 9
Particles, 24
Periodicals, 48, 65–7
Persian, 11
Phonetics, 41, 73–8
Phrase books, 40, 47
Phrases, useful, 82
"Picking up" a language, 33–4
Polish, 12, 18
Politeness, 26
Portuguese, 7, 8, 9, 33
Pronunciation, 74–8
Provençal, 11

QUESTION and answer, 61–4, 65, 66

RADIO, 40, 48, 72
Readers, 40, 46–7, 79
Records, 40, 48, 68–70, 71
Redundancy, grammatical, 25
Rhythm, 74
Romance languages, see Latin languages
Rumansch, 11, 12

Russian, 8, 9, 12, 18, 41, 43, 83, 87, 96

SAKHALIN, 11
Scandinavian languages, 12, 18, 84, 99
Semitic languages, 12, 41
Sentence construction, 12
Sentence drill, 36, 53–60, 65, 66
Sentence patterns, 83–5
Serbo-Croat, 18
Slavonic languages, 12, 18, 33, 41
Sound correspondence, 18–19
Sounds, 12, 13–15, 73–8
South America, 9
Spain, 11
Spanish, 7, 8, 9, 17, 18, 33, 60, 63, 81, 83, 84
Speech, organs of, 77
Stimulus and response, 37, 61
Sumatra, 10
Swahili, 9, 10
Swedish, 15, 17, 34, 58–9, 63, 90
Switzerland, 9, 11
Synthetic languages, 24, 89, 97
Syria, 9

TAPE, 36, 66, 68, 70–2
Textbooks, 13, 40–4, 53–60, 79
Thailand, 10
Tones, 15, 41
Translation, 4
Turkey, 9
Turkish, 9

UNITED Kingdom, 9
U.S.A., 9
U.S.S.R., 9

VOCABULARY, 12, 13, 15–21, 40, 42, 65, 79–83

WELSH, 11, 59–60, 63, 73, 81, 84, 87, 93
Word order, 22
Words, 15–21